A Little Book About Hockey

Written by Tao MacLeod

About the Author

Tao MacLeod has been involved in the world of sports media for several years, as a trained photographer, with experience of writing sports articles and covering events such as the Hockey World Cup and EuroHockey Championships. He has contributed to a number of publications and outlets, including website The Hockey Family, The Hockey World News and The Reverse Stick; Global Hockey Podcast. In 2019 he set up his own sports media website and then latterly podcast called the Half Court Press.

Tao is also a qualified sports coach, with a B.Sc. in Sports and Exercise Science. Having coached football in New Delhi, India, Shenzhen, China and Mexico City, he's now working in Edinburgh, Scotland. Since September 2021 Tao has been a youth team coach for Inverleith Hockey Club, having previously been the Youth Convenor for Waverley Inveresk Trinity Hockey Club. This is his first book.

Cover page photo credit; Tao MacLeod

Chapters

Introduction   Page: 5

Chapter One; Origins of the Game
    History   Page: 8
    Club Hockey   Page: 10

Chapter Two; Women's Hockey
    History   Page: 16
    Sexism in Sport   Page: 19
    Big Events/Moments   Page: 24
    First World Cup (Women)   Page: 28
    First Olympics (Women)   Page: 30
    First British Women's
    Olympic Gold   Page: 32
    Top Hockey Moments
    of 2022   Page: 34

Chapter Three: International Hockey   Page: 40
    Summer Olympic Games   Page: 42
    World Cup   Page: 49
    Women's World Cup
    2022 Review   Page: 53
    Men's World Cup
    2023 Review   Page: 58
    History of the
    Commonwealth Games   Page: 64

Chapter Four; Tournaments
    What Makes a Good
    Sports Tournament   Page: 71
    Pro League
    My Issues with the Pro League Page: 78

Chapter Five; Hockey Development
    Hockey Pedigree   Page: 86
    Hockey Stadia
    Permanent and Temporary Page: 91
    How to Increase Hockey's
    Fan Base in Britain   Page: 96
    Can There Be a
    Different Kind Of Fandom? Page: 103
    The Importance of
    Club Hockey   Page: 107
    The Importance of
    Indoor Hockey   Page: 117
    Business and Sport   Page: 125
    Hockey Rivalries   Page: 132

Chapter Six - Coaching
    What Makes a
    Good Coach?   Page: 143
    Coaching Opinion; The
    Benefits of Small
    Sided Games   Page: 150
    Iconic Hockey Coaches   Page: 153

Recommended Read and
Relevant Websites   Page: 159

Introduction

Hockey is a glorious sport. It is something that can be played by all the ages and enjoyed in a family environment. There are many ways to participate, spectate and to enjoy all levels of this sport. Most people view it as a means of physical activity and occasionally as entertainment. However, it is not merely this, it can be used so much more. Hockey can be a method of community engagement, personal and professional development, industry and business growth and charity work, as well as child and adult education. Those with a coaching and team management mindset can also use it as an intellectual exercise with regards tactics, strategy, recognition of movement patterns and continuous adaptations. It can also be an indication of a culture and tradition. How the game integrates itself into the psyche of the communities that plays it can say a lot about how minorities are represented in that country, how women and girls are treated and how those with disabilities are engaged.

Hockey can be a method for personal rehabilitation, personal growth, entertainment that provides a unifying force and a distraction from difficult situations beyond one's control and a way to overcome adversity, personal demons and generally what divides us. Sport, especially popular activities, provides fantastic methods of helping people from a variety of backgrounds and with a variety of needs.

There is a general consensus amongst health professionals that positive mental health is one of the benefits from physical activity. The increased endorphins that are produced, enter the brain through the blood stream can help the participant to feel better. This is often described as a natural high. The increased social activity, which comes from sports participation and is necessary in team sports, such as hockey, can also stop people from becoming insular and depressed, which is a risk for those who have been imprisoned, political or otherwise, as well as those who are at risk of being a vulnerable person within society.

Additionally, many community organisations, youth groups and sports clubs are recognising the positive impacts that team games can have on the wellbeing and lives of those who have been, or are at risk of becoming disenfranchised from society. Grassroots hockey is the term generally used for the development of a physical activity at its base, the lowest part of the game's pyramid, normally youth teams, but also the amateur adult participants, athletes, teams and clubs. It can have a fantastically positive effect on any given person and the communities that they live in. Participants are able to develop what can be described as soft skills. These attributes include communication, teamwork and social skills, as well as providing a focus on self-improvement, an increase in self-confidence and allowing individuals to become involved in a positive group setting.

Hockey has the potential to be many things, a form of entertainment and a method of exercise for many people. It can also be a method of education and rehabilitation. It has the potential to improve not only the outlook, but also the lives of the people involved. In this book we will explore a variety of different aspects of the sport of hockey, including its history and evolution, the inclusion of its participants, as well as some suggestions for its development. It is a mix of some of my previously written online blog posts, that have been compiled with some newly written articles. In general it is a celebration of a sport that I just find fun. I hope that you find the book enjoyable.

Tao MacLeod
August 2024

Chapter One - Origins of the Game

History

Human beings have looked for ways to be active and to compete against each other since forever and a day. We have been playing games since, I would imagine, we could stand upright. Over the centuries there has been a variety of sports that are similar to the what we now call field hockey. Historical artwork has been seen that depicts what may have been a stick and ball game being played in Ancient Greece roughly five centuries before the birth of Christ. There are similar activities shown to have been played in Ancient Egypt, Ming Dynasty China, Inner Mongolia and in the seventeenth century Indian region of Punjab. The Native Americans in the northern hemisphere played a variation of what is now called lacrosse, albeit this is a sport played mainly in the air rather than on the ground. To this day there are still stick and ball games being played in the Gaelic cultures of Northern Europe. The Gaelic Athletic Association of Ireland pride themselves on the game of hurling, whilst the Scots, in the north of Britain, play their own variation called shinty. Although, these two sports are predominately played in their respective countries of origin, there have been extensions abroad, based around overseas migration.

This is a story shared by numerous sports played in the modern era. Variations of many sports have been seen throughout history. When people talk about particular games being invented by the English, a more accurate description would be to say that they have been codified. In the mid to late nineteenth century, the upper and middle classes in England started to write down a common set of laws for sports such as rugby and association football. This allowed the various Public Schools across the country to bring together the various codes, variations and differing sets of rules that they all played by.

Mainly this was done in order to help with test matches and away fixtures between the teams, but also it would appear, to simply give the educated classes something to do in their spare time. The Public School system in England had developed an extra curricular education of sporting activities to promote their values of 'Muscular Christianity' within the pupils. Sport was used as a way for young men to exert themselves physically and help to prevent themselves from more sexual temptations before they could find themselves a wife. It was also noted at the time during the Boer War that the fresh recruits were lacking in strength and fitness, so the patriotic teachers of the time were decided upon the idea of training up their wards to fight for their country. The middle and upper class men within England were additionally keen to make use of their spare time. Codes were defined, rules were written and sporting clubs and associations were formed.

The students at Eton College were playing a type of field hockey during the mid-18th century and the first Oxford versus Cambridge varsity match was played in 1890. However, it is the club system for which the English are better renowned. This is a set up that has been copied and exported all around the world to varying degrees and has allowed domestic and grassroots hockey to have been developed in various different cultures and communities.

Club Hockey

Blackheath and Elthamians Hockey Club, as it is known today, claim that they are the oldest club in the history of the game, though this is disputed by Teddington. On their website, Blackheath provides a history of the club, which was linked with the local Rugby Football team until 1864, at which point the hockey club became its own entity. Blackheath became the trailblazers within the sport, having formed a hockey club in the first half of the 19th century, with their own version of the game that was similar to the rugby that they had been playing at the time. This was fifteen a-side, with a rubber cube used, instead of a spherical ball, presumably because it bounced at odd angles as a rugby ball would. The positions were also set out similarly to that of the sport of the parent rugby club, with a certain amount of hacking allowed. Hockey at this point in its history was played exclusively by men.

The oldest article in this club's possession is a book with records the minutes from a meeting 1861 in which the subscription was noted as being 7/6 and the retirement of secretary, Mr. R. O'Neil. The club notes that they have seen an external source that backs up their claim to having been in existence since before then, having been formed no later than 1840. The sport's close associations with education remained true here, with a strong allegiance being developed between the Rugby Football and Hockey Club and the locally based Blackheath Proprietary School, drawing players from the educational establishment to join the ranks of amateur participation. Blackheath's website goes on to describe an early flavour of what hockey would have looked like at their club,

"Then, as now, the game that Blackheath played bore occasional resemblance to other peoples. The club played on the heath by the All Saints church next to Montpelier C.C. and the game started when ten people were present. A sack containing about 35 caps, red one side and blue the other (hence the club colours today) was produced from the "Princess of Wales", and as more people arrived they joined in. The pitch was at least 180 yards long, 60 to 70 yards wide and the goal was 10 yards wide; there were no nets and a good surface was unnecessary. Teams were fifteen a side; a goalkeeper, two backs, two three quarter backs, three half backs and seven forwards and the ball was a cube of solid rubber "not to exceed 7 oz in weight" which had frequently to be boiled to keep it elastic. Sticks were made of oak bent by steam with a flat back, originally both sides of the stick could be used.

Within a remarkably short time however certain rules were introduced which have a modern flavour. In 1863 "Left handed hitting and throwing of sticks to be prohibited"; "that the hands and legs should not be used for stopping the ball at Hockey (goal keepers excepted)", this rule was later rescinded. In 1864 a player "shall not loiter between the halfway flag and the goal of the opposite side unless the ball be between him and the opponents goal". So by 1864 there was an offside rule, no feet and hitting with one side of the stick only; there was also a roll in and a hit out."

Cricketers also seemed to be pushing the sport of hockey forward, as an alternative to playing football during the winter months. Teddington Cricket Club created a hockey wing to their activities in 1871. They formed the basis for the rules of the modern game as we know it today, by introducing the shooting circle at either end of the pitch and changing the focal point from a rubber cube to a spherical ball. It was also the Teddington cricketers that used eleven players per team, as opposed to the version favoured by Blackheath.

Teddington make the rival claim to being the original hockey club. Founded in 1871, at least three decades after the game played in Blackheath had taken root, members of the Teddington Cricket Club were decidedly looking for a sport to play during the winter season. They decided to play a stick and ball game based along the lines of association football, instead of the rugby football style of game preferred by Blackheath. The Teddington Hockey Club website describes the evolution of thought better than I ever could,

"The TCC [Teddington Cricket Club] members rejected a game played by a Blackheath club that involved a 7oz (200g) rubber cube; catching, marking and scrimmaging; generally based on rugby football. The Teddington club chose to limit the number per side to eleven, and preferred to play with old cricket balls. They also introduced the idea of the striking circle ('The D'), and they played several games in Bushy Park, in the winter of 1871.

In defining the rules this way, Teddington were the first to play the game that became modern hockey. Clubs were also set up in Richmond and Surbiton in

1874, and inter-club matches were played between them and Teddington. The game grew sporadically, as the clubs didn't always agree on the rules!"

The sport of hockey was becoming more and more popular. Other clubs had started to spring up around England and by the latter part of the 19th century, there was even a working Hockey Association. The presence of an over arching organisation for the sport of hockey in England meant that by 1876 a set of rules helping to codify the game was written. The Hockey Museum website quote the following as an early piece of regulatory code,

"Rule 7: the ball may be stopped, but not carried or knocked on by any part of the body. No player shall raise his stick above the shoulder. The ball shall be played from right to left, and no left, or back handed play, charging, tripping, collaring, kicking or shining shall be allowed."

This was a definite move away from the game that had been developed by the Blackheath Rugby and Hockey Club, that seems to have been prone to a tad more physicality. These were first steps towards what we now consider the modern game. This original Hockey Association didn't last very long and soon disbanded. However, another and more successful attempt to organise hockey on a wider scale was achieved. On an evening in January of

1886 six clubs got together in order to form the Association that has evolved into the one we have today in England. Those original six were Teddington, Surbiton, Wimbledon, Trinity College Cambridge, Molesey and Ealing. Blackheath, who had been having difficulties with adjusting to differing rules when playing games against external opposition, finally joined in the early 1890's. The Hockey Association was formed in 1886, with The All-England Women's Hockey Association being formed nine years later in 1895.

Chapter 2 Women's Hockey

History

Women's sport has often seemed to be a second thought to many people. England and to a larger extent the United Kingdom, laid the early foundations of formalisation of many sports, in particular field hockey, including codification and the initial organisation of infrastructure. As discussed in earlier chapters, the early incarnations were all set up originally by men. At the time of hockey's beginnings, it was only men, and just the upper and middle class men at that, who could vote and enter politics within the UK parliament at the time. It wasn't until the year 1918 that certain women over the age of 30 could vote in a British General Election. It was another decade before this barrier to democracy and power was lowered to women over the age of 21. If you were born female in Great Britain in the time period that hockey was being developed your opinion was clearly deemed to be of less worth than that of a man, or even a boy.

The first ever women's team came into existence at least 16 years after the first men's team, if you consider Teddington to be the sport's forbearers, but potentially more than four decades after Blackheath started playing their version of a stick and ball game. Molesey Ladies Hockey Club were formed in 1887. Based in the Royal Borough of Elmbridge, Surrey, in the south of England, the twin towns of East Molesey and West Molesey are based on the south bank of the River Thames. The geography is important here, as the development of hockey in these early years was very much based in the regions in and around London. 'Moulsey Hurst' is also an early site of the sport of cricket, with East Molesey Cricket Club being based in the area, suggesting a further link between cricket and hockey.

The Irish were one of the earliest National Governing Bodies to introduce a women's team to the international scene. The Irish Ladies Hockey Union was established in 1894, a year after the Irish Hockey Union was formed. It developed out of a meeting at Alexandra College, a Church of Ireland private school for girls. The two separate hockey unions remained separate for over a century, when the International Hockey Federation decided in 1998 that only one governing body should run hockey in each country, prompting the merging of the gendered associations in the year 2000.

Over in England, the Ladies' Hockey Association changed their name to the All England Women's Hockey Association (AEWHA) in 1896. Women's hockey continued to develop on the international stage. Ireland carried on with their push for international recognition, when they hosted England in Dublin in 1896, winning out by two goals to nil. They also gave the Scottish women their first ever run out in the same city, five years later, beating their Gaelic cousins by the same score line. The Scottish Women's Hockey Association (SWHA) was set up at the turn of the century, in the year 1900. The organisation began in Edinburgh, after eight clubs came together that February to formalise women's hockey north of Hadrian's wall. This came several months before the Scottish Hockey Association (SHA) was set up on November 18, 1900, which focused on the men's competitions. The two organisations finally merged together in June of 1989.

Women's hockey moved overseas. In 1923, Belgium sent a ladies team to Lille, to play France. It was the central Europeans who came out on top of what was a low scoring game, winning 1 - 0. They then hosted their neighbours, the Netherlands in 1926 for the away team's first ever women's international match, winning 2 - 1 as they did so. The international Federation of Women's Hockey Associations was formed in 1927. This prompted further developments in the women's game, with more and more fixtures being arranged. Australia travelled to Cologne to give the German ladies their first taste of hockey at this level. It was a long way to travel for the tourists however, as they lost 3-2.

The German's, themselves, gave the Spanish ladies a chance to get their first game under their belt in 1936. The Spanish were taught a lesson, by the German's, who ran out 11-2 victors. Even within British shores women's hockey kept growing. In 1938 a match between England and Wales ladies teams was covered on the television. In 1951, England hosted Ireland in what was the first ever women's international fixture to be played in the prestigious Wembley Stadium. However, in terms of top level international competitions, the women's game was still left in the dark for a long time. It wasn't until 1980 that women's teams participated in the Olympic Games for the first time. European recognition took even longer, when it wasn't until 1984 before women participated in the EuroHockey Championships.

Sexism in Sport

The last decade, or so, has been a fantastic one for sports fans. The London 2012 Sumer Olympics seems to have become something of a cultural reference point for people in the UK. Similar to the impact of the Italia '90 World Cup for football in England, the hosting of a successful Olympic Games appears to have emboldened people to allow the spectacle of sports entertainment into their lives to an even greater extent.

We've had a deluge of sporting events on both terrestrial and pay-per-view television. The former has been showing some varied forms of sporting entertainment, partly due to the latter placing a lot of the larger and more popular events behind a paywall. As somebody who is interested in what all sport has to offer, I have enjoyed the deviation from the norm. Something that has stood out for me is the advancement of women's sport on our television screens. There has been a greater focus on women's football, hockey and basketball, in addition to the access we have normally been given to athletics and tennis.

As I mentioned earlier, I have an interest in what all sport has to offer. I am interested in how the showing of sports in the mainstream media can help move things forward and can have an impact on sports development. Men's football has had fantastic coverage for decades and the players, coaches and assorted personalities have benefited from the sponsorship that this attracts. I am, however, all for a more diverse sporting culture. The role of the media can be an important platform in the promotion of sports to the people. By grandstanding certain games, codes and activities it gives them credence and promotes physical activity, as well as the investment of money through the buying of television rights from broadcasters and providing a chance for advertisement. Thus the sports are allowed to grow. It can also provide role models for children and young people.

I have been particularly pleased to see more women's sport on television. Females have a higher rate of drop out from sport than males. One of the issues has previously been a lack of gender relevant role models in sport. Another issue is the way that female athletes are portrayed differently in the media from their male counterparts. Young women and girls who play regular sport often find that they are being bullied and/or made to feel insecure about the way that their bodies become stronger and more muscular. The way that sport makes them look doesn't always conform to the socially acceptable way that women and girls are told that they should look by advertisements, the media and other sources within society.

Advertisement campaigns and endorsements may have gone to the so-called 'attractive and aesthetically pleasing' female athletes, potentially limiting the earnings of many professionals who don't conform to gender norms and socially constructed ideas of attractiveness. It is important to break down these issues, firstly by confronting them and secondly to go about changing attitudes. These viewpoints will change with continued media coverage, showing off the talents at the high-end level, but also by people (men as well as women) standing up and lending their voice to be a part of the solution.

Over the years, there are many ways that women and girls are generally put down in sport. Due to the levels of ignorance that seem to be commonplace, it is easy to be disappointed with many things. I once heard a professional football coach say that the reason women are more susceptible to ACL injuries was due to the weight of their breasts, instead of the more accurate physiological reasons regarding the angles of the hips. I have picked up on certain other issues. Some people seem very comfortable in stating the visible differences in standard between men's and women's football, whilst ignoring the history of misogyny and withholding of finances, or not knowing the reasons why these things happened in the first place. The Dick, Kerr factory ladies football team is an example of how women's sport had the rug pulled from under its feet in the twentieth century. This doesn't help in any shape or form and can easily to be addressed.

There is an impatience to allow women's sport to develop in order to catch up with the men's games. A lack of top quality coaches, due to financial disparities between men's and women's sport and lack of opportunities at grassroots level, have put women's sport on the back foot. If this can be discussed and analysed in a public sphere, such as through broadcasting and other journalistic outlets, then we have a greater chance of providing our young women and girls with better opportunities to play and participate, as well as improving the standard of sport across the board. Thankfully things seem to be changing for the better, with greater public consciousness of women in sport and the top athletes being celebrated, but we still have some dinosaurs and misogynists out there with outdated perspectives. There is still a way to go in terms of breaking down barriers and finding methods to bring about equal pay.

There have been similar issues in the sport of hockey. Although we have a broadly equal game on the face of things, there have been similar financial hurdles for women to navigate compared to men. A huge money earner for male players has been the Indian Hockey League, while there hasn't been an equivalent for women until only recently. The inaugural event for the Women's Euro Hockey League (the European Cup for club teams) was only held in 2021. This might be surprising for many hockey fans, who assumed that the genders are on an equal playing field (or astroturf in hockey's case), within the sport. It was won by Dutch team Den Bosch, which is perhaps less surprising, but why wasn't this done earlier? Additionally, there were only four teams that season, with eight teams competing in 2022. When compared with the men's event, which had ten participating sides at that time and has been firmly established for many years, it shows that we can take nothing for granted and that there are still issues to deal with.

Big Events/Moments

Hockey at Wembley Stadium
Women's hockey internationals 1951 to 1991

First England Women's Fixture at Wembley
England 6 - 1 Ireland
03 March 1951
Attendance; 30,000

There had been an annual traditional of hosting a women's hockey international match in London. The All England Women's Hockey Association arranged test matches which became quite popular. 1,809 spectators came to a game at Old Deer Park, Richmond, in 1923. By 1935 8,600 tickets were sold for a fixture between England and Scotland at the Oval Cricket Ground.

This trend continued after the Second World War and an agreement was reached with Sir Arthur Elvin, the chairman of the Wembley company. The AEWHA would have to guarantee a minimum of 20,000 bums on seats. They duly succeeded, as a crowd of 30,000 turned out to watch the England ladies team run out six one winners over the travelling Irish national team. It was such a good turn out that it started an annual tradition for the English women to play at the stadium every March that continued for the next four decades.

First Foreign Team Wembley Fixture
England 11 - 0 Belgium
14 March 1953
Attendance; 43,000

The Wembley era test matches were predominately between the hosts England and other members of the Home Nations (Wales, Scotland) and neighbours Ireland. However, Belgium were the first side to come from outside of these islands to play under the famous Twin Towers. The game itself was a bit one sided, as the English ran out eleven nil winners, but it started a trend that saw other countries come over as well. In total ten different countries, from outside the British and Irish Isles, played against England in this stadium, providing some varied entertainment for the avid hockey fan. Touring teams included South Africa, the USA, Australia and the Netherlands with who the England and Great British sides would develop quite the rivalry with several decades later.

First Televised Wembley Fixture
England 5 - 1 Scotland
13 March 1954
Attendance; 45,000

This match is notable for being the first time a women's International was televised in its entirety on British television. The televisual spectacle didn't detract from having a large crowd. The game was also notable for attracting the highest gate to the Wembley fixtures up until that time, with a 45,000 crowd setting a record for number of spectators for the event. The home side ran out winners by five goals to one.

Largest Crowd for Wembley Era
England 3 - 0 Scotland
13 March 1976
Attendance; 68,000

The English versus Scottish rivalry seems to have appealed to the hockey fans of the time. The largest crowd to attend the Wembley era of test matches peaked in the mid-1970's, with 68,000 turning up to watch hockey under the old Twin Towers. The home supporters would have been pleased to see their side secure a three goal win against the Scots.

HM The Queen Attends Fixture
England 2 - 1 Wales
21 March 1981
Attendance; 62,000

One of the most notable moments of the Wembley Era of test matches happened one spring day in 1981. The chief guest for the game was the Queen, Elizabeth Windsor. Pre-match, she toured the perimeter of the pitch, in an open top Range Rover, greeting the crowd of hockey fans. Whether she would have been pleased with an English victory in this all British affair is not common knowledge, however it definitely would have been a memorable occasion in the careers of the players.

Final Wembley Era Match
England 1 - 2 France
16 March 1991
Attendance; 17,000

This fixture in the final decade of the twentieth century also bade a farewell to the matches at the Wembley Stadium, in North London. A major contributory reason for this decision was that the sport of hockey had, by this time, established itself on synthetic-based purpose built pitches and the long grass of the football field had become rather outdated. However, the two one loss to the French meant more than just the result of an international fixture. The Wembley era had become an annual showcase for the spectacle of women's hockey. We also saw a number of historical changes to the game, including the move away from positional labels on the back of shirts and the introduction of player numbers. The stigmas around competitiveness and financial rewards that came with the amateur mindset of the Edwardian period were broken down. The forty year period of international fixtures here also saw the introduction of team trophies and individual awards, as well as team and pitch side sponsorship.

The era of Wembley Internationals became more than just a series of games. It has become representative of many other things. A historical timescale of the sport can be seen throughout this time period, towards the modern version of the game that we see today. The loss to France in this final fixture also saw the loss of something more special - the loss of an annual spectacle for, not only hockey, but women's sport as well, something that was very important considering the time period that we are talking about.

First World Cup (Women)

The Hockey World Cup, as an event, didn't begin until the 1970s. Although, it took a few years before women were included in the concept, we didn't have to wait as long for equality as with the Olympic movement. In fact the inaugural women's competition was held in 1974, an entire six years before we saw female hockey players at the 1980 Moscow Games. Again, similar to the men's tournament, the women's World Cup took a while before it settled down into a regular pattern. It wasn't until after 1986 that we saw a four year cycle between iterations. It is a tournament that has gone on to be dominated by the Netherlands. Their women's teams have shown themselves to have a particularly world class programme, succeeding consistently in the sport's world championships. Other top teams have included Germany, Australia and Argentina, who have all performed to a high level, creating exciting rivalries to entertain the fans.

In that first World Cup, in 1974, we saw ten teams compete against each other on the French Riviera. The venue was in the coastal town of Mandelieu-la-Napoule, which is just south-west of Cannes and is known for having a fourteenth century fortified castle. Two groups of five teams played a round robin style first round, where each country played four games. Belgium, India, Mexico, the Netherlands, and Spain, were all drawn into the first round Group A. India topped the table, with the Dutch ladies coming in second place, due to the tie-breaker rules as both teams won three and lost one of their games. Over in Group B, Argentina, Austria, France, Switzerland and West Germany were pitted together. Here, the West Germans topped the group, with four wins from four, whilst the Argentines came second, having won their other three matches. In the Semi Finals, we saw the group runners-ups come out on top, with Argentina beating India and the Netherlands getting over the top of their rivals West Germany, both games finishing 1-0. Whilst the West Germans took the Bronze medal, it was the Dutch who came out as the first ever women's World Champions of hockey, winning 1-0 again, against the Latin Americans.

As mentioned earlier in this chapter, the Netherlands have gone on to dominate women's hockey over the intervening years. In the fifteen World Cup tournaments that have been held since 1974, the Dutch have won nine of them. In fact there has been only one occasion when they haven't medaled at all, which was in 1994, as they have also secured four silver medals and a bronze over the years.

First Olympics (Women) 1980 Moscow

The 22nd Olympiad of 1980 was notable for several reasons. It was the first time the Olympics were to be hosted in a Slavic speaking country, as well as a communist one. The host city was the Russian city of Moscow, which was a politically sensitive decision. Many Western nations boycotted the Games. Political theory rivals the United States led a protest over the Soviet Union's invasion of

Afghanistan. Several athletes (of individualised sports) from the 68 countries did, in fact, participate but did so under the Olympic Flag, instead of their nation state. However, many of the events that involved team participation had reduced numbers, based upon decisions made by the relevant National Governing Bodies and Federations. It was also the first time that the women's field hockey event appeared at the Olympic Games.

As only six nations entered teams into the women's competition, the decision was made to have just a group stage event, without any knockout rounds. This went against normal format of a first round group stage followed by a straight knockout series of matches. In this alternative set up the host nation Poland, Austria and India all finished outside of the medal positions. The Soviet Union, finished third with three wins from five. Czechoslovakia claimed second place, with three wins and a draw. The first ever women's Olympic champions were Zimbabwe, who didn't lose a game over the six day event, with victories over Poland, the Soviet Union and Austria. Not only were they the first ever women's first champion, but it was to become the African country's first and only gold medal, to date.

First British Women's Olympic Gold

August 19, 2016
Summer Olympic Games
Deodoro, Rio de Janeiro, Brazil

Women's Hockey Final
Netherlands 3 - 3 Great Britain
(Penalties; NED 0 - 2 GB)

This fixture had some form prior to the tournament, with the Dutch having lost to the English side in the final of the 2015 EuroHockey Championships in London, prompting a bit of a rivalry. However, the Netherlands were still favourites for the tournament having won the Olympic Games in 2012, as well as the World Cup in 2014. Both sides qualified for the Quarter Finals by topping their respective first round groups undefeated. Here, the Dutch got past Argentina 3-2 and then beat the Germans on penalties in their Semi Final match. The British found themselves playing the Spanish in their Quarter Final, who were dispatched 3 - 1, and then got over the top of New Zealand 3 - 0 to set up the Grand Final as a repeat from the year before.

The Final itself was a right old ding dong of an affair, famously postponing the BBC news so that the huge and unexpected UK TV audience could continue to watch the game uninterrupted. The British knew that it was going to be a tough encounter, but one that they could win. English winger, Lily Owsley, gave Britain an early lead after ten minutes, but this was cancelled out shortly afterwards, as Kitty van Male equalised for the Central Europeans. Former World Player of the Year, Maartje Paumen then gave the Dutch the lead in the 25th minute, however this only lasted for a few seconds, as Christa Cullen levelled the score to make it 2 - 2 at half time. Kitty van Male gave the Netherlands the lead again shortly after the break and the Dutch looked set to take home the trophy, but in the 52nd minute Nicola White scored a third for her side to set up a penalty shoot out. Here, the British goalkeeper, Maddie Hinch, came into her own, with her now famous notes. The goalie was spotted on camera reading bits of information on the opposition that she kept on the side of her drinks bottle. It seemed to work for her, as she denied all of the Dutch penalties, prompting the British to win 2 - 0 with Helen Richardson-Walsh and Hollie Webb (now Pearne-Webb) scoring the all important penalties to win the Olympic Games for the first time since the men in 1988 and the first time ever for the women's side.

Top Hockey Moments of 2022

As women's hockey becomes viewed more and more in the mainstream, the year of 2022 saw twelve months of memorable hockey. We had several international tournaments including the Commonwealth Games and the Women's World Cup. There was a variety of memorable sporting moments for fans and players alike to remember. Here, we look back in celebration of some of the best of what this sport has had to offer so far...

Women's Hockey World Cup - July
Netherlands 3 - 1 Chile
Francisca Tala scores against the Netherlands

In what became one of the most fun and heart-warming stories of that summer, this moment made many within the hockey community smile. The World Cup was held during July and saw debutants Chile add to their hockey history in a unique way. The Latinas had become a neutrals favourite during the early stages of the tournament, with their charismatic coach and swashbuckling players. Before the tournament Francisca Tala, a senior forward within the team, scored a good goal during a training session. One of her friends in the side dared her to do it again, but when it mattered. As the draw for the World Cup had already been made, the South American champions knew that they had a tough encounter ahead of them. A bet was made that if she scored against 2018 World Champions the Netherlands, then Francisca would have to marry her boyfriend. A phone call was made, the man in question was informed and nothing more was thought of it. That was until their first round match against the Dutch.

As per usual, the Netherlands dominated most of the games that they played in. They had beaten the Irish by five goals to one, before getting the upper hand over their Central European rivals, Germany, three-one. Chile, on the other hand, had mixed fortunes up till this point. They had lost their first match against the Germans four-one, but were able to win against Ireland, with just one goal between the two sides. Denise Krimerman had scored both of the goals for Las Diablas. Throughout the first two games, Tala's boyfriend had been one of the more vocal Chilean fans, with the TV cameras repeatedly finding him and his friends in the crowd.

On the 6th of July, the two sides met in the last match of Pool A. The Netherlands took an early lead, through Lidewij Welten in the 14th minute. The typical hockey fan might have thought that this would be it, game over, and that the Dutch would run away with things. However, just after the start of the second quarter the Chileans come forward. An attack down the left wing, saw the ball sent towards the goal. A miss trap from a Dutch defender saw the ball pop out into space. Francisca found herself with the ball on the end of her stick, in space, at the back post. It was easier to score than to miss and she duly found the equaliser. Her team mates surrounded the goalscorer, reminding Tala of the bet that she had made with them. The Dutch went on to win the game by three goals to one, but the Chileans celebrated like they had won, lifting their forward onto their shoulders, much to the bemusement of their opponents.

Women's Hockey World Cup - July
Netherlands 3 - 1 Argentina
Felice Albers's goal against Argentina in Final

The Netherlands, as expected, dominated the World Cup throughout the earlier rounds. They have taken home more World Cup titles in the women's game than any other national team. They won every one of their games, scoring 17 goals in the process. Everybody knew that they would be favourites to maintain their world title. The only team that seemed able to get in their way were the Argentines. Having been drawn on opposing sides of the tournament, the two best teams in the world met in the Grande Finale.

It was a game of fire and ice. The Dutch with their ability to maintain discipline within the ranks, against the passionate attacking flair of Argentinas Las Leonas. Hockey fans around the globe tuned in to see who would come out on top. Would the Latin

Americans be able to break down Holland's solid press, or would the World Champions win yet again? It was the team in orange who won the day and did so in style. They dominated almost every minute of the final, running out three-one winners, with Augustina Gorzelany's goal coming merely as a 46th minute consolation, after the game was all but done.

It was in fact the third and final goal for the Netherlands that was the standout moment of the game and possibly the tournament. It was a goal that showed Dutch hockey at its best, in terms of technique, team work and individual dynamism. The Argentines looked to press their opponents high up the pitch, early in the second half. The score was only two-nil and if the Pan American champions could knick one they would fancy themselves to stage a comeback. The Dutch found themselves in a tight spot, in the bottom left hand corner of their defensive quarter, with their opponents ready to pounce. However, a quick combination between three players, with the brilliant Eva de Goede acting as the playmaker, they were able to move the ball forward along the sideline. De Goede fed Freeke Moes in space. She was able to cut inside to her right and drive past a defender's weak side and over the half way line, with a beautiful first touch and a drop of the shoulder. With her second touch Moes released Felice Albers down the right wing. Albers carried the ball into the circle, cutting across Valentina Costa as she did so, before calmly placing the ball past Belen Succi, in the Argentine goal. It was a world class goal, from a world class team, performed at the pinnacle of the sport.

Commonwealth Games (Women) - August
England 2 - 1 Australia
England win hockey gold on home soil

The Australian hockey team were favourites for this tournament. They have medaled at every one of the Commonwealth Games hockey tournaments since the inaugural women's event in 1998. They had won the gold medal five times, including at the previous event, held on the Gold Coast. The English were on home soil, but most neutral fans would have pegged the Hockeyroos for the win. Undaunted, however, the English had their own plans.

Organised and disciplined throughout the match, England created chances for themselves through pluck, spirit and teamwork. Having won a free hit in a deeper position near the half way line, Holly Hunt squared the ball to Laura Unsworth. The experienced playmaker saw Flora Peel's lead to the right wing and played it up the sideline. Peel took a touch and centred a pass into the circle. Somehow it found Hunt (who had started the move), unmarked and in plenty of space. She had time to pick her head up and bury her shot into the goal to open the scoring. Four minutes later, Flora Peel was involved in England's second. Playing a combination off from the Australian baseline, she found herself at a 45 degree angle to the goal, within shooting range. She fired a cross-come-shot at the far post, where Tess Howard was waiting to deflect it home.

Rosie Malone got one back for the Aussies, in the last minute of the game, but it was only a consolation goal. England's women won their first ever Commonwealth Games title and in front of a home crowd to boot. Additionally, it was broadcast on the BBC, allowing a greater number of fans see a successful hockey team in action. For the older players in the squad, it would also represent a happier memory than that of losing to the Aussies in the final of Glasgow 2014 on a penalty shootout. This victory was well deserved.

Chapter Three International Hockey

After the incubation period of domestic club hockey players, fans and governing bodies were starting to develop an interest for a different type of challenge. It was no longer enough to play the team from the neighbouring hamlet, town, or county. People wanted to view matches on the international stage. Strangely, considering their development of the game thus far, the English didn't get in there first. The first ever international hockey fixture was between Ireland and Wales (men) in Rhyl in 1895, with the Irish running out winners with three goals to nil. England's men played their first ever game in the same year, against the Emerald Isle, at Richmond, which the Anglo-Saxons won five nil. It wasn't until a year later, in 1896, until the first ever women's international was played. Again this was played out by England and Ireland, but this time in Dublin with the home side winning two nil.

All of this additional action led to the formation of the International Rules Board, in London, in 1900. This not only helped to codify the rules across national boundaries, but seemed to help drive the sport forward and through state lines. Scotland's women played their first game in Dublin, losing two nil to the Irish. France's men joined the fun for the first time, hosting England in Paris in 1906, losing three nil. Two years after this though, the sport of hockey took an important and historical step forward in its development on the world stage. Hockey appeared at the summer Olympic Games for the first time in 1908. We'll look at this festival of sport in more detail later in the book, but this is an event that has become culturally significant within the game.

It took several years before an international governing body was established. In 1924, the Fédération International de Hockey (FIH) was finally set up, 16 years after the sport first appeared at the Olympic Games. The founding members of this organisation were Austria, Belgium, Czechoslovakia, France, Hungary, Spain and Switzerland. There seems to have been a shift away from English and British hockey authorities here, as those on the continental mainland of Europe started to take further ownership of their participation. The organisation is still around today, as the main organising authority of the game. The FIH's website tells us a bit of their history and progression over the years,

"By 1964, there were already 50 countries affiliated with the FIH, as well as three Continental Associations - Africa, Pan America and Asia - and in 1974, there were 71 members. Today, the International Hockey Federation consists of five Continental Associations, 137 National Associations and is still growing."

Women's Hockey seems to have been developing at an arms length to the men's game to a certain extent. Although the original incarnation of the FIH was founded by representative nations that fielded both male and female teams, women went on to take control of their own futures. In 1927 the International Federation of Women's Hockey Associations (IFWHA) was formed. It wasn't until 1982 that the FIH and IFWHA came back together as an overarching international governing body.

Summer Olympic Games

1908 London

The 1908 Olympic Games were held in London, between the 27th of April and the 31st of October, setting a record for the longest games of the modern era. The fourth Olympiad was originally scheduled to be held in Rome, but after Mount Vesuvius erupted in 1906 the Italian authorities re-directed the previously earmarked funds from their Olympic preparations in order to support the devastated city of Naples. Great Britain put her hand up to offer an alternative to the International Olympic Committee (IOC) and the city of London got to host the first of the three Olympiads to be awarded to the British capital city, thus far.

The Olympic Games of 1908 were notable for several reasons. Controversies included the

American team refusing to dip their flag in respect and deference to the British Imperialist monarch, King Edward VII, during the opening ceremony. Also, for some reason, the Swedish flag wasn't displayed above the White City Stadium, therefore the Swedish team went home. Additionally, in the early part of the twentieth century, Finland was considered to be a part of the Russian Empire, and therefore the athletes were expected to compete under the Russian Flag, as well as display it when they paraded into the main stadium. The Fins, who weren't overly happy about being ruled by a foreign force, decided not to carry a flag at all and presented themselves to the King of England without a banner.

The events of the 1908 Games also prompted codification of standard rules for sports, as well as the selection of judges, referees and umpires coming from a variety of locations, instead of just from the host nation. The organising committee had decided to judge the running events using the British standard rules system, instead of the International rules. The obvious happened when an American runner, called John Carpenter, was accused of interference with a British runner in the 400 metre race. The definition of interference was different under the two different systems and thus helped to cause a problem.

Many people may know of the games for what happened in the marathon. The athlete who had initially won was the Italian Dorando Pietri, who had metaphorically and almost literally busted a gut to take a strong lead as he approached the end of the race. However, this over exertion had caused quite a negative effect on him physically. With only two kilometres to go, Pietri began to feel the effects of dehydration and fatigue and started to struggle. Umpires had to help him for the first time, as when he entered the stadium he took the wrong path. He fell down several times as he approached the finish line and was helped back to his feet. His final time was two hours and 54 minutes, however, it took Pietri ten minutes to go the final 340 metres. A complaint was lodged and he was disqualified, meaning that American Johnny Hayes took first place instead. Due to the unfortunate nature of his disqualification, Queen Alexandra presented Pietri with a gilded silver cup the next day.

Most importantly for hockey, though, the 1908 Olympiad saw the introduction of the sport as an Olympic event. Unfortunately, it was men only at this stage, as it would be several decades before the women joined the festivities. Here, the Home Nations competed separately, instead of as Great Britain. Only six national teams competed in this inaugural tournament; England, Scotland, Wales and Ireland, as well as, France and Germany. England got over the top of France by 10 goals to one in the first round, whilst Scotland beat Germany four nil, in what was the first ever international game for the Central Europeans. Although they lost, they got to have their second match in quick succession. What appears to have been an unofficial fifth versus sixth playoff match was put on the following day, for the losers of the first round. Germany beat France one nil. England played Scotland in the first of the semi finals, coming out on top as six one winners. In the other game, Ireland guaranteed themselves a medal, by beating Wales three goals to one. As there was no Bronze Medal Match in those days, Scotland and Wales shared third place. England came out champions of the first ever Olympic Hockey Tournament, with a resounding eight one victory over the Irish, in the Grande Finale.

1920 Antwerp

Hockey wasn't involved in the Olympics again until 1920, which was hosted in Antwerp. This may seem like a bigger gap than it perhaps should, due to the global disaster of the Great War (1914 to 1918). In fact the only Games to be played out was the fifth festival, which was held in Stockholm in 1912. The sixth Olympiad was held two years after the end of the war that was supposed to end all wars. The Central Powers, who were on the losing end of the conflict were, as a result, banned from competition.

These were the first Games where doves were used to symbolise peace and that saw the use of the Olympic flag. The Russians themselves were not invited to take part in the Games as part of its political embargo by the West. Argentina, the Kingdom of Serbs, Croats and Slovenes, Brazil and Monaco competed for the first time at these Games. New Zealand, who had previously competed as a combined entry with Australia, sent their own team this time.

Finland, who had gained their independence from Russia in 1917, were competing under their own flag for the first time. They finished a respectable third overall, taking 15 Gold Medals and 34 overall. The Japanese team had some difficulties. They almost didn't make it home. They had raised enough money for the trip to Belgium, however they ran out of money for the return journey. They managed to gain sponsorship from Japanese based companies Mitsubishi and Mitsui in order to return back to their homeland.

The hockey event was held at the Olympics Stadium, which had a capacity of 30,000. Only four teams entered this time around. Denmark, France, hosts Belgium and Great Britain. It was, in fact, England who were competing as representatives for team GB. This was the first time that a group system was set up, instead of a straight knock out format. Each team played the other once, meaning three games each. Denmark won two of their three games, with results over Belgium and France. Belgium's only win was over France, who finished bottom of the four team pool. Great Britain topped the group with three wins from three. They got over the top of Denmark five goals to one, then a resounding 12 - 1 victory over Belgium. The French gave the British a walkover for their final game of the tournament. There wasn't a knock out stage to this event, meaning that with France finishing in last place, Belgium took the bronze, Denmark the silver and Britain the second gold in a row.

Men's hockey was dominated by the Asians for the next several decades. The sport had been taken to India by the British Army. They took to the game like a duck to water. In the thirteen Olympiads between 1928 and 1984 they won the hockey event eight times, also taking a silver and two bronze medals, easily becoming the most successful men's hockey team at the Summer Olympics. Post partition, Pakistan won it a further three times, who also took the silver medal three times and a bronze once in this time period.

Pakistan have placed second in the all time medals table, behind their close neighbours and rivals, India, beating out Europeans Great Britain and Germany in terms of specific medals gained.

In terms of women's hockey at the Olympic Games, there aren't as many statistics as for the men's event because of the limited number of tournaments that women have been allowed to compete. Apart from the inaugural event in 1980, that saw many national teams stay at home in protest of the Soviet Union's invasion of Afghanistan, the Netherlands have participated in every tournament since. The Central Europeans have had quite a strong hold over women's hockey over the years, as we will see further when we talk about the World Cup tournaments, but they have had a record breaking show of fortune across the Olympiad. In the eleven Olympic events held for women, the Netherlands have medaled nine times; three gold, two silver and three bronze. The Dutch reached the Grande Finale five times in a row, winning in 2008, 2012 and 2020(21) losing in 2004 to Germany and only missing out to Great Britain in 2016 on penalty shuffles.

World Cup

There has been fifteen World Cup tournaments for men's hockey teams. These competitions were initially dominated by Pakistan, who had brought their Olympic form to these events. The Asians medaled six times in the first eight competitions, four gold, two silver (including a loss to rivals India in 1975) and a solitary fourth place finish, after losing to the West Germans in the 1973 playoff match.

Starting in 1971 the World Cup was initially held every two years, before settling into the now standard four year cycle from 1978 onwards. The inaugural tournament was hosted in the Catalonian/Spanish city of Barcelona by local hockey club, Real Club de Polo, who's facilities were also used for the 1992 Olympic Games. Ten men's teams participated in 1971, spread across two groups of five teams.

Group A was made up of Argentina, France, India, Kenya and West Germany. Each team played the other once. The Indians won all four of their games, to top the group and qualify for a semi final game against whoever finished second in Group B. Kenya and West Germany both finished on four points apiece and therefore had to play off against each other to see who would advance, with the Africans coming out 2-1 winners.

Across in Group B, things were a bit more straightforward. Spain finished in top position to advance to a Semi Final game against Kenya. Pakistan, who finished on the same points tally as the Spanish, came second, due to the head to head records in their earlier game. This set up a tasty match against India in the Semi Finals.

The Spanish needed to go to extra time to beat Kenya by one goal to nil. In the other game, Pakistan came out on top in this derby match, beating the Indians 2-1. In the third place playoff, India got over the top of Kenya, 2-1, after extra time, to take the Bronze medal. In the Grande Finale, Pakistan took revenge over their Group B rivals, Spain. After losing the first round match against the Europeans, the Pakistanis came out as 1-0 winners to win the first ever men's World Cup.

The top goalscorer for the tournament was Tanvir Dar, with eight goals. Born in the Indian city of Amritsar, in 1947, he moved to Pakistan after Partition, eventually dying in the capital city of Lahore, in 1998 aged 50. He had a fairly successful hockey career in his short life, having also won the gold medal at the 1968 Olympic Games and the 1970 Asian Games.

Although, it took a few years before women were included in the concept of a Hockey World Cup, we didn't have to wait as long for equality as with the

Olympic movement. In fact the inaugural women's World Cup was held in 1974, an entire six years before we saw female hockey players at the 1980 Moscow Games. Again, similar to the men's tournament, the women's World Cup took a while before it settled down into a regular pattern. It wasn't until after 1986 that we saw a four year cycle between competitions.

In that first World Cup, in 1974, we saw ten teams compete against each other, on the French Riviera. The venue was in the French coastal town of Mandelieu-la-Napoule, which is just south-west of Cannes and is known for having a fourteenth century fortified castle. Two groups of five teams played a round robin style first round, where each country had four games. Belgium, India, Mexico, the Netherlands, and Spain, were all drawn into Group A. India topped the group, with the Dutch ladies coming in second place, due to the tie-breaker rules as both teams won three and lost one of their games. Over in Group B, Argentina, Austria, France, Switzerland and West Germany were pitted together. Here, the West Germans topped the group, with four wins from four, whilst the Argentines came second, having won their other three matches. In the Semi Finals, we saw the group runners-ups come out on top, with Argentina beating India and the Netherlands getting over the top of their rivals West Germany, both games finishing 1-0. Whilst the West Germans took the Bronze medal, it was the

Dutch who came out as the first ever women's World Champions of hockey, winning 1-0 again, against the Latin Americans.

As mentioned earlier in this chapter, the Netherlands have gone on to dominate women's hockey over the intervening years. In the fifteen World Cup tournaments that have been held since 1974, the Dutch have won nine of them. In fact there has been only one occasion when they haven't medaled at all, which was in 1994, as they have also secured four silver medals and a bronze over the years.

Although, it took a few years before women were included in the concept of a World Cup, we didn't have to wait as long for equality as with the Olympic movement. In fact the inaugural women's World Cup was held in 1974, an entire six years before we saw female hockey players at the 1980 Moscow Games. Again, similar to the men's tournament, the women's World Cup took a while before it settled down into a regular pattern. It wasn't until after 1986 that we saw a four year cycle between competitions.

Women's World Cup 2022 Review

The Women's Hockey World Cup 2022 was the first time that such an event was hosted in two different countries, the Netherlands and Spain. It is an interesting concept, but one that might need a bit more thought. Some of the teams were having to travel in a short space of time and with the current climate crisis, I'm not sure if the balance was quite right. There were also issues with attendances, which we'll come back to later on. It was also the first Hockey World Cup that I was able to watch fully on the television, which seems like a bit of progress, although it would have been interesting to have it on state television in order to help gain a wider audience.

The main thing that struck me in this tournament was how similarly the varying national teams played to each other. There are some cultural differences of course; the Argentines are keen to run with the ball, using individual skills, as do the Indians. The Dutch use their midfield to move the ball and create angles, for example, others like to attack more than defend or the other way around. However, most teams play a variation of 4-3-3/3-4-3. The main differences between the teams are to do with the levels of funding for the respective programmes. The professional teams are a step above in terms of players, depth of talent, skill execution and consistency compared to those who are broadly semi-professional, or amateur.

The two teams who made it to the final match, the Netherlands and Argentina, were the top two ranked sides in the world. They were placed on opposite sides of the draw, due to the competition's seeding process, in order to keep them away from each other in the early rounds. A similar intention was shown in the Tokyo Olympics; the men's Gold Medal Match also had the two top teams in the world face off against each other. They do the same thing in football, presumably to sell more hamburgers and fizzy pop drinks at their World Cup through advertising, but it rarely ever happens in the same way. It's almost a cliche at this point to talk about the two best teams meeting in the semi final of football tournaments. This is because the professionalism of the men's game has brought the competing nation's much closer together in recent years. There are more shocks, due to the tactical nuances that decades of fully funded league structures can bring.

This isn't the case in hockey. The team's who are ranked lowest in the tournament tend to finish towards the bottom, rarely have we ever seen an Irish success in 2018 and we probably won't see such a repeat again until there's more consistency across the various domestic set-ups throughout the different domestic competitions.

In the latter half of the World Cup tournament, we saw several classification matches take place, in order to rank the various teams from 16th to 10th. I like this, it provides a clearer idea of where each team sits in the story of the competition, it also gives the lower grade teams more chances to get international experience and FIH world ranking points. In the context of the invitational tournaments such as the FIH Pro League and such, many teams like Ireland, South Africa, Japan and so forth, don't get the same opportunities to develop and progress themselves. The only issue was the classification matches didn't provide enough of an incentive to strive for, sometimes creating stale and stagnant matches. I would propose a secondary championship for those who go out before the quarter finals. A World Plate, or Trophy would give players, coaches and teams an incentive to strive towards those higher positions and provide more entertaining matches. This might also attract more spectators to games and perhaps even more sponsorship and endorsements for the athletes.

This also ties into my final point about the World Cup this year. Outside of the matches that involved the two hosts, Spain and the Netherlands, the games were poorly attended, particularly in the Catalonian venue of Terrassa. During the bidding process for the hosting of competitions like this, world and continental championships, qualifying events and so forth, the FIH should be encouraging, if not mandating, National Governing Bodies (NGBs) to create better fan cultures within their domestic leagues. If England Hockey, for example, wanted to host a World Cup again, they should be told to entice more spectators down to their league games and help in the general and specific areas of developing a culture of watching hockey in the build up to the larger international events. This would then provide greater footfall through the ticketed gates and, in theory, create a better atmosphere within the stadia. School kids and youth team players should be allowed in for free, or heavily discounted prices. When I was coaching girls football in Edinburgh, the Scottish Football Association would send wads of free tickets to all of the local clubs with women and girls teams, whenever the Scotland Women were playing a match. This got more people down, including families and groups of friends of all ages. Another method would be for the national federation to hold competitions and giveaways for people to win tickets to matches and thus fill out the empty seats that we see at various elite level competitions.

Aside from these points, I thoroughly enjoyed the recent World Cup. It was great to see several world class players competing against each other; Gigi Oliva of Spain, the Granatto's of Argentina were delightful, the entire Dutch side was brilliant in the Final, culminating in a truly spectacular goal to finish the game. There were some lovely stories and personalities on show as well. The Chilean coach Sergio Vigil comes across as a lovely man and one of his players, Francisca Tala, proposed to her travelling boyfriend after scoring against the Dutch. Moments like these are what make up the stories that come with tournaments and sport. I can't wait for the next competition to enjoy.

Men's World Cup 2023 Review

The fifteenth edition of the men's FIH Hockey World Cup was held in 2023. Watching as a fan, remotely from a television in Scotland, hosts India seemed to put on a good show. This festival of hockey, this sporting championship, provided plenty of entertainment. We saw comebacks from early deficits, skill, tactical battles and goals aplenty. It truly was a window in to the best of what the sport of hockey has to offer…

Grande Finale & Bronze Medal Match

Germany 3 (5) - (4) 3 Belgium
Gold Medal Match

Let's start with the outcomes of the tournament. Germany won the Grande Finale in a penalty shoot-out five shuffles to four, after a tense match that saw the lead change hands, culminating in a three all draw. Belgium took an early lead, through two field goals in the first ten minutes from Florent Van Aubel and Tanguy Cosyns. The Germans had made a name for themselves in this tournament as the comeback kings. They found a late equaliser in their Quarter-Final against England, winning on penalties, before netting a last gasp winner against Australia in the Semi-Final matchup between the two sides. They carried on this storyline in the Gold Medal Match, scoring penalty corners in the second and third quarters, from Niklas Wellen and Argentine-born Gonzalo Peillat, setting up the final fifteen minutes with a two-two scoreline.

Germany took the lead for the first time two minutes after the break, through their captain Mats Grambusch, who bagged their only field goal of the game. They probably had hoped that this would be enough, but Belgium forward Tom Boon scored a late equaliser for Belgium in the 58th minute, forcing a penalty shoot-out tiebreaker. This in itself was a tense affair. After four shuffles, the score was three-two to Germany. Belgium got one back through Kina Antoine taking the game to sudden death. Niklas Wellen and Florent Van Aubel both scored for their sides, but it was on the seventh round that we found a winner. Thies Prinz tucked his away, whilst Tanguy Cosyns (a goalscorer from earlier in the game) wasn't able to convert. Belgium lost their crown, having held it since 2018. This was the first time that Germany had won this tournament since they hosted the World Cup themselves, in Mönchengladbach in 2006 and their third title in total.

Australia 1 - 3 Netherlands
Bronze Medal Match

In this Bronze Medal Match, the Netherlands secured their fourth World Cup medal in a row, having finished second in 2018 and 2014, as well as an additional third place position in 2010. It was the Australians, however, who took the lead. Jeremy Hayward opened the scoring from a penalty corner in the twelfth minute. The Aussies came into this tournament ranked number one in the world, however, losing a Semi-Final (only on penalties) and then this third place playoff saw them drop down to fourth place. The Dutch staged their comeback in the third quarter. Their equaliser came in the 32nd minute through a Jip Janssen set piece. Thierry Brinkman then added a couple of field goals before the break, securing their two goal lead.

Observations of Teams and Fandom

It is always interesting to watch a tournament of this standard. Elite level competition can provide insights into tactics and strategies that are useful for grassroots coaches like myself. How to set a team up is a question worth thinking about whenever you watch the top teams play. Also, observing the skills used and decisions made by the best players in the world can be fantastic for helping youth team players improve their own performances. I was particularly impressed with how Germany played and how they used their team press. I also remembered how important it is to approach the shooting area at 45 degree angles, whist looking towards the back post, as well as driving towards and along the goal line, for a cut back, as an alternative. It seemed that a fair amount of the field goals were scored after the ball transitioned through these areas. The watching and analysing of these fantastic playing squads and athletes can help us to move the domestic game forward.

We still have moderately strong geographical cultural playing styles within hockey. It is easy to compare our sport to football, which has become much more global in its cross pollination of ideas. Football players and coaches have moved around the world a lot more freely over the years, due to the large extent of that game's professionalism. Hockey, in comparison, still broadly maintains its historical and traditional national identities that come across in playing styles. The Germans are quite organised, the Argentines are full of flair. The Indian hockey teams have broken the mould somewhat more recently. Traditionally, they produced individual players full of skill and attacking talent. However, I believe they have opened themselves up to ideas and coaching from other cultures and philosophies, giving them now a much broader approach to the game. I think that they have blended their brilliance in one-versus-one situations, with a pass and move approach normally favoured by the Europeans. It's very fun to watch. In fact, if I was to pay good money to watch a men's game of hockey, it would be an even contest between the Indians and the Australians, with their assertive and high tempo 'Gun 'n' Run' style of play.

In terms of shutting out contests, during the match itself, teams still don't seem able to control a game, dictate the tempo, or hold onto a lead very easily. This tournament has highlighted an issue in hockey, which has been around for a while. If a football team takes a two, or three goal lead, you can be fairly certain that a well drilled side will slow the game down, control the positioning of the ball and only speed up the play, if and when they want to. However, this isn't the case in hockey. We can almost expect a comeback from a team only losing two nil at half time. Germany came back from such a position several times, including the Grande Finale itself. Argentina missed out on a medal, because they couldn't hold onto a lead against a lower ranked South Korean side and they do, in fact, seem to try and slow the game down in order to dictate tempo. It's something to think about at least...

I do find the fan and spectator engagement with the World Cup interesting. Asking many of the players that I see around my club and elsewhere, there didn't seem to be many people within the sport watching this world class event. We could see this in the amount of bums on seats at the games. India, unsurprisingly, had the largest support during the tournament. Outside of when the hosts were playing their games, there wasn't a large crowd in attendance. An Indian classification match, after they had missed out on the medal rounds, had a better atmosphere, it seemed, then either of the Semi-Finals. This is common at most of the events around the world. We had a similar issue at the 2018 Women's World Cup in London. The only countries that have the potential to draw large crowds for the neutral games as well as their own fixtures, are Belgium, Germany, the Netherlands and possibly Argentina. All of these countries have a strong club system and a thriving domestic scene. Hockey fans are prevalent within the sporting culture in these locations. I'm led to believe hockey is one of the most popular sports amongst women and girls in Argentina, with Las Leonas garnering passionate and vocal support within that part of the world. The engagement of fans and the promotion of a strong domestic culture is how we can promote the sport.

If National Governing Bodies want to host a World Cup, continental championships, or even FIH Pro League and other test events then more can be done on this front. The federations and associations should be enticing club players to come along, through promotions and competitions. We should bus in school children and local youth team players for them to enjoy the spectacle (actually this is something that the Indians seemed to do well as hosts). Those who weren't watching, who didn't take in a game, or cast an eye across a television screen, surely did miss out. There was some great hockey on show, with some entertaining matches played throughout the tournament.

History of the Commonwealth Games

The twenty-second edition of the Commonwealth Games was hosted in the English Midlands City of Birmingham. 5,054 athletes, from 72 national teams, across 283 events from 20 different sports were in action from the 28th of July 2022, with the curtain coming down on the 8th of August. This was the latest version of a multi-sports festival that dates back to 1930.

The first ever edition of the Commonwealth Games went by a different name. The British Empire Games were held in Hamilton, Ontario, Canada. This was a much smaller edition to what we saw in Birmingham in 2022. Only 400 athletes competed in 59 events, across six sports. In this inaugural festival only 11 national teams came to Canada; Australia, Bermuda, British Guiana, England, Ireland, Newfoundland (who would later compete as part of Canada), New Zealand, Scotland, South Africa and Wales. The sports were Aquatics (Diving and Swimming), Athletics, Boxing, Lawn Bowls, Rowing and Wrestling. Women were included in this festival, but only in the aquatic events and were, in fact, hosted in a different accommodation venue to their male counterparts. Since then, the Games have been held on four year cycles, with only the 1942 (Vancouver, Canada) and 1946 (Cardiff, Wales) editions being cancelled due to the Second World War.

The Canadian City of Vancouver got their chance to host their Games in 1954, by which time the name had changed to the British Empire and Commonwealth Games. This was the fifth edition of the festival, which saw the 'Miracle Mile', where Englishman Roger Bannister and Australian John Landy both ran sub-four-minute races, in an event that was televised, for the first time ever, on live television across the world. Here, Northern Rhodesia and Pakistan also made their debuts in Commonwealth Games competitions. With further changes to social values happening over the years, there were further etymological changes to the name of the Games. By the time of the ninth edition in 1970, hosted in Edinburgh, Scotland, we were referring to it as the British Commonwealth Games, with the British reference finally being dropped by 1978, Edmonton, Canada.

There have been several controversies over the years, primarily centred around the Apartheid policies of South Africa. The second edition of the British Empire Games were originally awarded to Johannesburg, but was relocated to London. This was because the South African Government refused to allow participants of colour to compete. Nigeria boycotted the 1978 Commonwealth Games in

Edmonton, Canada, due to fellow competitive nation New Zealand's contacts with Apartheid-era South Africa. Eight years later, there were similar protests over the 1986 Scottish hosting of the Commonwealth Games held in Edinburgh, due to the UK Prime Minister Margaret Thatcher's support of South Africa at the time. This meant that thirty-two of the fifty-nine eligible countries, who were primarily from Caribbean, Asian and African nations, boycotted the competitions and saw the lowest number of participants turn up since 1950.

The Commonwealth Games has been dominated by the more financially secure and developed countries, sometimes referred to as 'Western Nations'. This can be seen by where the host cities and nations have been located. Birmingham 2022 will be the seventh Games hosted in the United Kingdom (England, 1934, 2002, 2022; Scotland, 1970, 1986, 2014; Wales, 1958). Australia have hosted five Commonwealth Games, Canada four, with New Zealand hosting three Games. The Asian continent have only hosted the Games twice, once in Kuala Lumpur, Malaysia, in 1998 and then in the Indian Capital City of New Delhi, in 2010. The Caribbean has only hosted the Games once and an African city has never been selected. This dominance can also be seen in the medal tables, however, one time this has seen a bit more of a global distribution. Australia, England and Canada, perhaps unsurprisingly due to their financial capabilities, have won more medals than any other Commonwealth nation. However, Asia and Africa are represented in the all-time top ten by India, South Africa, Kenya and Nigeria.

There have been several notable athletes over the years. The famous English actor Jason Statham has, actually, quite a strong sporting background. A participant in football, kickboxing and martial arts, he was also involved in aquatic sports. He represented England in the diving events at the 1990 Commonwealth Games in Auckland, New Zealand. The same year, BBC Sport presenter, Gabby Logan represented Wales in the Rhythmic Gymnastics event. Australia's most famous swimmer Ian Thorpe has won 10 gold and a silver medal, across two Commonwealth Games, in 1998 and 2002. Belfast born, Northern Irishman, David Calvert holds the record of attending the most Commonwealth Games, attending every festival between 1978 and 2018. Born in 1951, he is a shooter and has won four gold and four bronze medals. Scottish lawn bowler, Willie Wood and Isle of Man cyclist Andrew Roche have both competed in seven Games.

Hockey has been present at the Commonwealth Games since 1998. Men's and women's events were introduced at the same time, with Australia dominating the medal podium. In the men's tournament the Aussies have won the gold medal on all seven occasions. India have finished second three times (making them the best of the rest) most recently in 2022. England have taken the bronze medal a record four times. Forever the bridesmaid, three of the third place finishes for the English have come in the previous three Commonwealth Games.

In the women's competition the Hockeyroos have carried on their nation's success found by their male compatriots, however there has been a bit more diversity in success. Australia have won four gold medals in this event, with India (2002) New Zealand (2018) and England (2022) have also come out winners at the Commonwealth Games. The big hitters in the women's hockey tournament have been the Aussies, the Kiwis and the English, with seven medals each, if including the gold, silver and bronzes that they have picked up over the years.

However, hosting this festival of sport seems to come at a cost. The 2022 Commonwealth Games were only awarded to Birmingham after the South African city of Durban stepped back from its previously agreed hosting of the festival due to financial constraints. There is a huge up front commitment to spending and use of resources, which can be understandably off putting to many local authorities.

However, Durban's loss was Birmingham's gain as athletes, support staff and tourists from all around the world descended on the East Midlands, spending money and fuelling the economy. There are also the additional social benefits of people seeing new sports for the first time and finding inspiration for new activities. Additionally there is the investment made into facilities and national governing bodies in order to support their grassroots activities. The Birmingham festival were also the greenest, most environmentally friendly games ever, with a focus on renovation and sustainability.

Other countries and cities don't seem to see the positives in hosting such an international event. The Australian State of Victoria was meant to be hosting the 2026 Games. Sadly, they have since pulled out with the regional Premier, Daniel Andrews, stating rising financial costs as the reason for the change of heart. According to the BBC, the initial outlay was expected to be AUS$2.6 billion (£1.4bn, US$1.8bn). This was reported to have risen to more than AUS$6billion (£3.12bn, US$4.09bn), before the decision was made to pull out of hosting duties. There has been some suggestion, including from the chief executive of the Commonwealth Games in Australia, that these costs have been exaggerated, or could have been reduced. Comparatively, Birmingham 2022 was reported by the Independent to have seen £778 million spent by the British

Government. Be that as it may, since I started the writing of this book the Canadian province of Alberta has canceled its bid to host the 2030 Games. The costs, according to a BBC article were estimated to be at CAN$2.7 billion (£1.5bn, US$2bn), which were too high for the local economy to bear. This means that, at the time of writing, there are no current bidders for that particular festival.

This, I think, is a shame. The Commonwealth Games is something that brings people together from all over the world. As a spectacle, it allows sports fans to check out different things, create memories and develop a sense of prestige around certain venues. Additionally, as previously mentioned, it can help to develop infrastructure and grassroots sports. It also gives opportunities for athletes to compete at a higher grade than what is normally available to them. As the friendly games, the 'Commies' provide opportunities to amateur athletes to mingle with the elite of their particular code, or activity. This is often the pinnacle of the careers of many athletes, players and coaches. The experiences taken from this have the potential to raise the standards of participation in their respective domestic leagues back home.

Chapter 4 Tournaments

What Makes a Good Sports Tournament

We all love a good sporting competition, tournament, or championship. Spectators tune in for the stories, the tactical nuances and to see what the players and athletes can do. The big events on a global scale are the Summer Olympics, the football World Cup and the Tour de France. However there are also several smaller multi-sports events such as the Commonwealth Games, the Asian Games and the Pan-American Games. Fans and players alike look forward to these spectacles as they come around. What do they all have in common? What can the organisers of smaller tournaments take with them in order to promote their own events? Here are some thoughts from the author…

Competitive Games

It's important to have teams of similar abilities competing against each other. There will always be a type of differential in talent between groups of players, in fact that's part of the charm of an invasion sport such as hockey, or football. It's interesting to see how different groups band together in order to achieve certain objectives. A slight variation in ability can be interesting as teams or individuals will adapt tactics and strategy in line with their own capacity and that of the opposition.

However, too much of a gulf in class can allow the games to become ludicrously one sided, or uninteresting.

The FIH Hockey 5's tournaments, or EHF EuroHockey Qualifiers of 2022 are good examples of how not to arrange fixtures. Scores that are overwhelmingly in favour of one team over the other is not useful to the players, teams, or coaches involved. Nor is it interesting for fans and spectators to see what fundamentally amounts to a dead rubber. Games should be between teams that are close enough to challenge each other and for the under dogs to potentially cause an upset. The size of the event and qualification process should reflect this.

Opportunities should be given for lower ranked sides to develop their abilities, so that they can compete at a higher level in the future. This could be a mix of funding, coaching clinics and lower graded tournaments where players and coaches can gain greater levels of experience. The well established format of the EuroHockey Championships, I think, works well. The four-tiered system allows for a promotion and relegation set up on a two year cycle. This gives lower ranked teams something to strive towards and a chance for silverware. Those players who perform in the lowest division can still have a degree of success at international level and given chances to engage with their fans and teams are able to gain sponsorship aligned with their standard.

An Underdog Story

Fans like a surprise. The spectators want to see somebody who can take on the big boys and win. Just like the tale of David and Goliath, we enjoy an unexpected story about greatness from those that we least expect it from. Morocco, for example, at the 2022 men's football World Cup, defeated former European champions Portugal and former world champions Spain in order to become the first African team to reach the World Cup semi finals. It's a narrative that will warm the hearts of sports fans across the globe.

The 1988 Winter Olympics threw up a couple of underdog stories that have since been turned into movies. Michael 'Eddie' Edwards, was a plasterer from the English spa town of Cheltenham. He came in to snow sports later than most, after being introduced to skiing on a school trip at 13 years of age. He eventually moved across to ski jumping, competing at the 1987 World Championships. Due to the low bar set for qualification, he became the first British athlete to compete at the Winter Olympic ski jumping competition since 1928. Even though he came dead last, in both the 70 metre and 90 metre events, he won the hearts of those watching, earning the nickname Eddie the Eagle.

This was also the name of the biopic movie on his life and sporting career.

The Jamaican bobsleigh team also made their debut at the 1988 Calgary Olympic Games. The Caribbean islanders came in as true underdogs, even having to borrow some basic equipment in order to compete. Dudley Stokes and Michael White finished 30th out of 41 competitors in the two man event. In the four man competition, the team which included Stokes and White, as well as Devon Harris and Chris Stokes, crashed on their third run meaning a disqualification. However, the sight of them pushing their sled across the finish line showed grit and determination. Their story was told via the movie Cool Runnings.

Also, from the sport of hockey, there have been a couple of great anecdotes that can be added to the fables and folklore of the game. The Chilean women's hockey team, had a good showing at the 2022 World Cup. They took on the Dutch on their home turf, as well as some other big names, getting to the second round and bringing neutral fans along with them, with their charismatic coach and swashbuckling players. They finally placed an honourable 13th place at the tournament. One of their players, Francisca Tala, even proposed to her boyfriend on the side of the pitch, creating a rather memorable moment, as mentioned earlier in the book.

Additionally, the Irish team that that got to the final of the Women's World Cup in 2018, created a brilliant storyline. Coming into the tournament as the second lowest ranked side in the championships, they played above their seeding, getting all the way to the Grande-Finale. Their opponents that day, the Dutch, had been refusing to play test matches against them for sometime. The Irish coach, Graham Shaw, joked that they weren't able to turn them down now. Ireland secured their highest ever tournament position in their hockey programme's history, much to the delight of Irish fans and the friends and families of the players.

Accessibility for and Engagement with Fans

Prestige is a large part of what makes a tournament special. I have a thought that prestige essentially derives from the memories of fans, players and coaches. The media, including journalists and reporters, can help to increase, and/or caption these memories, but it is fundamentally created by those who are directly involved, either as participants, or as spectators. All things being considered, there are several things that tournament organisers can consider in order to make things easier and more enjoyable for fan groups, spectators and journalists.

Good stadia is essential. Accessibility for those with disabilities should be included for every newly built stadium. As should be food and drink kiosks (which can also be a method of earning money for clubs or federations), hygienic toilets and comfortable seating. Media suites for journalists, such as writers, photographers and videographers, as well as reporters are important for helping to tell the world what is going on at an event. Internet access (surprisingly not available at every venue that I've been to as a journalist) is useful for getting out scores and results, post match feedback and the ability to tell the stories that come from the competitions. The capacity to stream, or televise matches, with at least one commentator, allows for those to engage with the event from further afield than those within the local area. Bringing all of the action to as wide an audience as possible is important in order to create interest and increase popularity. An increase in viewership is an important factor is growing sponsorship and other revenue sources.

Fundamentally, the more people at the games throughout any given tournament the better things become for any given sport. Having greater numbers of fans inside the stadium, or venue, is what we want. Affordable ticketing is something that many clubs, federations and organising committees don't necessarily consider. The selling of tickets is an often used method of earning money for whoever is hosting the event. However, it is also important not to price people out of attendance.

Once people are through the gates money can be earned other ways, for example through food and drink kiosks, as well as replica kit sales.

The greater the number of attendees at a game, the better the atmosphere within the stadium will be, thus creating a more enjoyable spectacle. Having a range of prices for tickets could be a way of getting more bums on seats. Additionally, allowing school children, or youth team players in for free can raise the attendance levels quite easily. The Spanish hockey federation seem to be able to get large numbers of kids into their stadium on a regular basis, with audible benefits being heard during their televised matches. If these young fans enjoy themselves then they will potentially begin a life time of involvement in the sport.

Pro League

My Issues with the Pro League

There has been a lot of international hockey being played over recent years. The number of caps gained by players for representative hockey has increased since the eras of black and white photography. Some of this has been televised, on pay per view. In and of it self this is something to celebrate and enjoy. As a sport, hockey is a fantastic spectacle that can be enjoyed by a range of different sports fans. Its fast, exciting and requires high levels of technical skill and physical fitness in order for it to be played well. The invasion aspect of the matches often throw up flash points of attacking fun, as well as tactical intrigue. However, the tournament that is currently being pushed and shown on a regular basis is far from being perfect.

The FIH Pro League is the brainchild of the international governing body for the game and has been created in order to promote the sport. The standard of the matches has generally been decent and, at times, quite good, however it has also been beset with issues since its inauguration. Founded in 2017, the first season to be played was in 2019. It is a round robin competition played by international teams. The format has changed slightly, with small adaptations being made as we have gone along. The Covid-19 pandemic hasn't helped, but the tournament doesn't seem to have captured the imagination of the fans, at least not to a great extent, which seems to be the point of a promotional championship. Here are a few of my concerns with the Pro League...

Elitism

The Pro League provides a greater number of matches for the teams who are already playing at a high level. However, it doesn't do much to help growth of the developing hockey playing nations. The introduction of the FIH Nations Cup as a lower division has allowed promotion and relegation between the different grades, but we will have to wait and see if, in practice, this will be anything more than a token gesture. After South Africa declined their invitation to participate, having won the men's Nations Cup, concerns over the financial implications for national governing bodies have been raised. The African continental champions have an amateur programme, meaning that entering a team into a global league competition over several months was considered unaffordable. What is the point of having the chance, in theory, to be a part of something that is unattainable to those who are being shown the carrot?

It has become clear that the Pro League makes the richer teams better, without providing enough chances for the lower ranked countries to improve.

Instead of helping to grow the game of hockey, the tournament risks reinforcing a hierarchical system that will nullify competition at other global events such as the World Cup and Olympic Games. Rather than promoting hockey, we could see a disengagement from fans as they see the same few teams continuously win time and time again.

Media Production

The Pro-League TV show has been besieged with production and technical issues. Over the years I've seen team lineups that have shown 12 players, instead of eleven, some players with head shots, others without, some in their team's traditional colours with teammates in the alternate shirt. There has been a lack of consistency in style of imagery and presentation between the men's and women's matches, even on the same day. In a match I once watched, the England team line-up showed Shona McCallin as the reserve goalkeeper, when, in fact, it was Sabbie Heesh. McCallin isn't even a goalkeeper. In a separate instance Great Britain's Lee Morton's name was misspelt. England and GB were the home team on both occasions and, presumably had a Communications Officer talking to the production team. How do these mistakes continue to be made? Is it incompetence, or a lack of professional pride? If the whole point of the FIH Pro League is to introduce new fans to the players and the game, then it isn't particularly helpful that incorrect information is being sent out as a part of the pre-match graphics.

Carbon Footprint

As somebody who is also concerned about the environment and the current climate emergency, I am curious about the need to have teams and support staff jetting about around the world for just a few of games of hockey over a weekend. The latest format of the Pro League is what the FIH describe as mini-tournaments spread across a number of months. At the time of writing, the 2022/23 season was in action. Nine teams were competing that season, with matches having started in November of 2022 and the finals being played in July 2023. In this time matches were played in Latin America, Asia, Oceania and Europe. Effectively, large groups of people are travelling all around the world, over a period of seven months, for what amounts to nothing much more than a series of test matches. Is this worth adding to the planet's carbon footprint? Is the development of a minor tournament and a smattering of national teams, for our entertainment, worth the price of global warming? I would suggest not.

There are alternative formats that could be used that would reduce the harmful emissions associated with air travel. The use of venues that are accessible by train travel, or the team bus, for the majority of

National Governing Bodies would be a start. This is already done on a small scale, but when spread across such a long time period it is not going to have much of an effect. Therefore it would make sense to play games over a shorter period of time. The sport of hockey is already familiar to the concept of festival tournaments. The World Cup is often played over a fortnight. Continental championships take about eight days to complete with a similar number of teams involved as the Pro League. The most famous of hockey tournaments, the Olympic Games, is done and dusted within about three weeks. This would dramatically bring down the need to travel long distances for months on end.

Fixtures

The games have been sporadic, overlapped each other and occasionally poorly timed. Great Britain has both men's and women's teams competing in the respective gendered tournaments. There were a few matches during the month of June that have been scheduled for unusual times. A couple of the fixtures had been penciled in for 5.30pm on a Monday. Another one timetabled for 12.30 in the afternoon on a Tuesday. Who is able to watch matches at these times? How many fans would have been able to attend in person, or watch on the television? I would suggest that most people who would want to engage with this spectacle will have been at work, dealing with personal, or family issues, or otherwise engaged.

European football games are often played midweek, but at pre-specified periods of the season, after most people have finished work. Kick offs are often starting within a standard timeframe, allowing to create an expectation from those who wish to watch to make themselves available. This allows fans to return home, go to the pub with friends to watch a match, or arrive at the stadium to become vocal supporters. If the Pro League is meant to be promoting the sport, then the FIH should be suggesting similarly habitual push back times in order to help create a buzz around the events. This would help to maintain fan and media interest, therefore helping to grow hockey.

Waste of Resources

Participation in the Pro League evidently comes at a cost. Otherwise, as previously mentioned, South Africa would not have pulled their men's team out of the tournament. Travel and accommodation costs for players and support staff will add up over time. This is money that could be put to better use. The finances of governing bodies could instead be spent on domestic hockey, helping clubs to reimburse their players for time taken off from work. If we can create more part and full time players within national league structures then the standard of hockey will inevitably rise. Additionally, the money available could be shared around a greater number of federations, helping those outside the top ten to develop stronger national programmes, employ a greater number of coaches and generally create a stronger industry within the sport.

Conclusion and Alternatives

If the concept of the Pro League was to promote hockey, then, at the very least, it hasn't been doing this adequately enough. It takes valuable resources away from a sport that has a large amateur base. Also, in a time when we need to be thinking about how to reduce our negative impacts on the environment and strive towards being net zero, we need to be looking at ways to have a smaller carbon footprint when travelling to events. Fans also need to be engaged further. Too many of the games are on pay-per-view television, with fixtures being played at seemingly sporadic times and locations. There is also a desire to have greater opportunities for lower ranked teams to develop, to learn and to try new things in competitive situations. Therefore we need to create further chances for movement between the grades.

The Champions Trophy was an elite level event that was liked by fans and players alike. It involved the winners of the major tournaments qualified for this bi-annual tournament (a reformatted Pro-League could be an additional qualification route). It became something that was easily promotable and something that hockey enthusiasts willingly engaged with. It only lasted a short period of time and the centralised location helped to reduce unnecessary global air travel. A predecessor to the Pro League was the World League. This gave smaller hockey playing countries the chance to develop against teams of similar abilities, before advancing to the higher rounds to play against better opposition.

I quite like the idea of the Nations Cup, with its condensed format and the aim of winning promotion to the Pro League. Additionally, the EuroHockey Championships are graded into four divisions. Here the winners, as well as the runners up of a lower division gain promotion to the more prestigious event in two years time, with two teams moving in the other direction. This promotion and relegation system creates fan intrigue, media interest and the possibility of increased sponsorship. It is also a system that could be used in other tournaments that wouldn't be as elitist as the current incarnation of the FIH Pro League. The tiered system allows teams to play against those of a similar ability, meaning competitive games (good for development, television and supporter engagement). The games can also be played over any period of time that is thought of as appropriate. At least it's something to think about.

Chapter 5 Hockey Development

Hockey Pedigree

It's about time that the British celebrated our history within the sport of field hockey. It is about time that we highlighted our pedigree within the game and the broader communities of physical activities. It's about time that we showed the non-hockey fans what they are missing. Other sports talk endlessly about what has happened in their respective codes and games. Football, for example, has many books, magazine articles and television programmes dedicated to its progress and development. In North America, in particular the USA, they discuss very little else apart from the sports which they invented. Baseball, American football and basketball, seem to have a special place in many an American sports fans imagination and memories of occasions both big and small seem to be sentimentalised during one's lifetime. In Britain, the birthplace of what we now know as field hockey, there is very little pride in what we have done, what we have achieved thus far. Between the men's and women's national teams we have won three EuroHockey Nations Championships, two Olympic Games, a number of minor international tournaments as well as a variety of medals (including gold) at Commonwealth Games and World Championships.

I think that part of the issue is that many of our successes have been overseas and away from home, out of the public eye. Until recently there has been very little for the British hockey fans to sink their teeth into. Compared to other sports, such as rugby and football, the elite level hockey leagues within the home nations don't offer much in the way of a spectacle. Primarily the entertainment comes from the international scene, which has been by and large hosted in other parts of the world. Only recently has an interest been spiked in the English/British hockey national teams. I think that the turning point in the mainstream sporting consciousness was when the ladies XI won a bronze medal at the 2012 London Olympics. A euphoria of sporting patriotism during the Games gave the sport a platform across the country. The public awareness of hockey has increased slightly in the time since, partly helped with further success at major tournaments, but six years is a comparatively short time for sports fans to get sentimental about the game. Additionally, somebody who is not already involved in hockey is unlikely to attend a game as a spectator.

As a fan of English football, I perhaps have a rose tinted viewpoint of Wembley stadium. It is a temple of sport. It is the home of English football. A place of historical significance that draws a broad spectrum of people through its gates. Wembley has hosted both the finals of the 1966 World Cup and the 1996 European Championships, plus countless domestic and continental cup competitions, including the Stanley Matthews Cup Final. It was also the stadium where FC Barcelona won their first European Cup, and where many Auld Enemy games have been played. I have never actually watched a game of football at Wembley, even still, it is undoubtedly a cherished and important part of sporting life within the UK, because of what has happened on that turf.

Other sports have similar sporting shrines. Rugby has Twickenham, Basketball has Maddison Square Gardens, Baseball has Yankee Stadium, Tennis has Wimbledon, where a certain Andrew Murray has had the occasional success. The English hockey equivalent of these wonderful places is the Lee Valley Hockey and Tennis Centre. It is a new venue that was built as part of the London Olympic legacy, as such it is still quite a new facility and hasn't had the time to build up the history and the aura that other stadiums have. It has hosted a few tournaments thus far. The most significant perhaps when England's ladies won the EuroHockey Nations Championships that were held there in 2015, followed up in 2018, with the Women's World Cup. This is exactly the sort thing we need in order to boost the sports public image of the sport.

What we need more of are the major events that stay in the consciousness and memories of the fans.

This would give greater emphasis to the importance of hockey. It is the fans and spectators that provides value with regards the standing of sports in the public consciousness. The way to get fans to think fondly about hockey is to give them opportunities to have a good time at events that are based locally to them.

Additionally, the hockey federations and national governing bodies within the home nations need to be more pro-active in creating fans at club level. I once watched a streamed feed of the England Play-Off Semi-Final, at Lee Valley Hockey Centre. The attendance was pretty low for such a high level game at this point of the season. When I was coaching girls football in Edinburgh, the Scottish Football Association would provide tickets for women's international matches to local female clubs so that coaches and players were more likely to attend, thus promoting the women's game. If the England Hockey Board can foresee that attendances are going to be low, that they aren't going to be selling the tickets anyway, then what's the harm in sending tickets to local schools, to hockey clubs based in London, provide spare tickets for the players involved in the game itself for family and close friends. By raising the attendances pro bono in the short term, then the hockey authorities can create a larger fan base that is invested in the sport, creating better atmospheres at games and potentially increasing the pool of players and creating positive gains in the long term. By giving people the opportunity to spend time at hockey events, both large and small, with their friends and family, then those spectators will value the sport in greater depth. They will remember what happened in particular games that they were not directly involved in as players and help to create a living memory of the sport itself. This is how we both celebrate and create pedigree within hockey, so that it can be seen on a par with the more mainstream sports played and watched in the UK.

Hockey Stadia - Permanent and Temporary

In the previous section, we looked at how to develop the sporting pedigree of hockey. Here I discussed the developments of the sport within the public consciousness, when compared to other games, such as rugby, football and tennis and so forth. I concluded that we needed to create more tangible moments within the stadiums available to us in order to create a sense of collective memories and therefore prestige within the perspective of a wider audience. This has actually been happening to a certain extent. Since hosting the 2015 EuroHockey Championships England Hockey has hosted the 2018 Women's World Cup, as well as put on home Pro-League fixtures for the England and Great Britain sides at the Lee Valley Hockey and Tennis Centre - all except for a small numbers of fixtures one year, but more on that later. Additionally there were four games as part of the men and women's GB teams as part of their Olympic Qualifying campaigns, for Tokyo 2020(21).

Hopefully this sort of elite level of competition in London will continue. It will mean that the relevant media outlets can promote hockey, the players can bring the fans back in numbers and people can create their own culture within the stadium. This will take time, perhaps several generations to bear the sort of fruit that I'm writing about, but it's at least a start. Other sporting arenas have particular atmospheres; going to the rugby is different to the football and both have different ambience to that of the tennis. For example, you may get kicked out of Wimbledon, if you behave like you might do at Wembley. Due to relevant lack of mainstream attention and amateur status of the domestic game in this country the undercurrents and overtones inside the national hockey centre can be quite tame.

What has happened recently, though, is that a new type of hockey turf has sprung up and come to the forefront of the sport. During one of the early Pro-League campaigns, the Great Britain teams opted to move their home games to The Twickenham Stoop, which is the stadium of Harlequins Rugby Club. Of course, the field is made of grass, which is not used at international level anymore. A temporary turf was laid down for the matches. This was in order to supply a larger facility for the demand for tickets. This is a great initiative, I think, as a way of promoting the game.

Although, the idea of moving around the country (or just across the city of London, in this case) is brand new for field hockey, it has precedent in other sports. Squash has been played in front of the Egyptian pyramids, for example. The use of a transportable court seems to provide some fantastic images. Additionally, while Wembley stadium was being rebuilt, the England men's football team went to many different football clubs here, there and everywhere. I once travelled to see to see an international fixture at Old Trafford and that wasn't the only place that was used. The women's team has been doing this for a while.

It makes sense to move the national team around the nation. By doing so, a national governing body could actually help to promote the sport in question in a variety of counties and regions, as well as make money in other areas of high demand. This temporary turf concept would allow this. It could also have a mutually beneficial financial impact for both the national governing body and the host club, with tickets being sold, as well as food and drink stalls open to the general public. I saw a discussion topic raised on social media, asking why the Great Britain team rarely, if ever, came to Scotland and Wales to play games. In the thread of responses it was pointed out that some of the non Anglo-Saxon players probably deserved a chance to play within their own home nations. This type of representation could tweak at the threads of fandom within local communities. So, there are definitely benefits to this new concept.

Hockey Ireland obviously thought it was worth a try. In the build up to Tokyo 2020(21) their Olympic Qualifiers for the women's team were played at the Energia Park (home to Leinster Rugby), making use of the 6,000 capacity stadium. They laid down a temporary turf for these two games. Coming off the back of the women's team successful World Cup in 2018 it allowed for promotional actives to encourage spectators turn up. During the very same Women's World Cup in London, the England national team was selling out the Lee Valley Hockey and Tennis Centre (10,000 with temporary seating). This obviously made an impact on the decision to go to the Twickenham Stoop, which can fit 14,800 people inside. The 'supply and demand' thought process that has been taken on board with both Great Britain and Ireland is good to see and will help to grow the game.

What I am worried about, however, is that fans and players alike won't be able to develop a home atmosphere for the team that they support and play for. The Lee Valley Hockey and Tennis Centre is one of the best field hockey facilities in the world, which the players seem to enjoy playing at. In order to develop this sense of homeliness, this concept of pedigree and a stadium name that becomes a byword for the sport itself, then we need a focal point to base it around. That, unfortunately, wouldn't make use of these fantastic new temporary pitches. Surely a balance between playing important matches in one place and having other events spread around the country would be something that can happen now, in big time stadia! This way we can have the best of both worlds where the national team can belong to everyone, but we can build upon the enjoyment for people to come to the national stadium.

The Pro-League could be an answer to this. It would allow for some games to be played here and others to be played over there. I believe that the Australian hockey teams do something similar and it seems to work for them, especially as they have fans spread out across such a vast land mass. Let's wait and see what happens, but there is plenty of potential for success here.

How to Increase Hockey's Fan Base in Britain

Hockey is a great sport. It requires skill, power and team work. When played at its best it can be fast and entertaining. It's also one of the more progressive sports out there in terms of opportunities for both men and women. Hockey is also played all around the globe with teams from the Oceanic, Asian, European, Pan American and African federations within the top twenty of the FIH World Rankings. However, there isn't enough engagement with fans and spectators of the sport. Not enough is being done, within the home nations of Britain to increase the spectacle of the game and for it to become more viewer friendly. Here are some ideas for hockey to become more accessible to the general public across England, Scotland and Wales.

Clubs and Domestic Hockey

Hockey games should be more enjoyable for fans. Currently, if somebody wanted to watch their local side, or a friend or family member play, then they tend to have to stand for the duration of the fixture whilst exposed to the elements. Being that the domestic season is played during the winter months, this isn't going to be much fun for the average sports fan in Britain. Seats and shelter should not be too much to ask. For clubs that own their own facilities, providing a certain standard of comfort can be quite straightforward. Planning permission can be awarded to a community sports organisation, as most councils should be quite encouraging towards such activities. Teams that play on community pitches and school turfs might have some difficulties. However, there's no reason why arrangements for temporary seating can't be arranged on the sides of the pitch. Also, gazebos and tenting can be put up in order to provide some protection from the wind and the rain to those who have come out to support their team.

Additionally, for those who are based at schools on a regular basis, pre and post match entertainment can be arranged, with some element of communication and forethought. Engagement with the school's drama and/or music departments and extra curricular groups can, not only create more of a buzz around the side of the pitch but, bring more people to the game. When done in addition to the organisation of food and drink kiosks and other market stalls, a greater hubbub and sense of community can be created, as well as the potential for additional revenue streams for the club. This doesn't need to be done every week, but once a month or even once a season, perhaps when both the men's and women's first teams are playing at home and could be a constructive way of developing a culture of attendance of matches.

Attendance of Matches

Many of the elite level matches are ticketed, especially at international level. It's not unreasonable to expect people to pay some amount of money for sporting entertainment. As long as there is a certain level of comfort and accessibility is provided from the organisers, clubs, or federations, it's perfectly acceptable to ask for some dosh in return. However, a range of prices should be available. Many fans feel like they are priced out of watching international hockey, with several of the England and Great Britain Pro League matches being played in front of broadly empty stadiums. This shows that people are hardly queuing up to watch the national team play in a mid level tournament at the prices they are being asked to pay by England Hockey.

At the EuroHockey Qualifiers, hosted by Uddingston Hockey Club and Scottish Hockey (in August 2022), tickets were priced quite low, at around £5 on the gate. Turnout was relatively high, in particular for the final Scotland fixture on the weekend, which saw a sell out crowd come down to support the home team. This shows me that the fan base is out there, as long as the events are marketed properly. It also indicates that the overpricing of tickets can be prohibitive at this stage of the sport's growth within the United Kingdom. A balance needs to be found here. Yes, ticketed events are a way for hockey clubs and federations to earn some much needed monetary income, but there should be a sliding scale of pricing for entry to the venue. Additionally, I think that allowing school children and youth team players to enter for free is a positive long term policy for developing a fan culture. When I was coaching girls football in Edinburgh, whenever the Scottish Women's National Team was playing in town, the Scottish Football Association would send out free tickets to all of the local clubs with girls and women's teams. Parents would take their children to matches and create a positive family atmosphere within the stadium. Additionally, at the matches that I attended, I saw groups of teenagers socialising and enjoying the atmosphere together. This is a perfect method to allow young fans to participate as fans and spectators on their own term. This engagement with the local community is a method that could be copied in hockey. Competitions for people to win tickets could also be a way to entice people down to watch more hockey and engage with potential sponsors, willing to put some money in the sport.

International Games

As mentioned previously, England/Great Britain Hockey introduced a new concept to the international hockey scene, just before the Covid-19 pandemic. One of the latter Pro League fixtures of the first season of the tournament was played at a neighbouring rugby stadium, in London, on a temporary astroturf pitch. This was laid down for the weekend, over the top of the established grass field with all of the necessary equipment and hockey furniture transported for use for the duration of the event. Although this temporary field was only sent down the road from the national stadium, it did prompt a conversation about how this technology can be best used for the development of hockey and the greater engagement with fans around the country.

Why not take hockey on the road? These matches were hosted at the Stoop, home of Harlequins Rugby Club, but why not go to a football, or cricket stadium in the North of England, a rugby club in Wales, or to a sports venue in Scotland? The Australians and Argentines have been playing their Pro League fixtures at different locations each time, why can't England/Great Britain do the same thing here? It doesn't need to be restricted to the Pro League either. The Great Britain Elite Development Programme (GB EDP) is basically the Under 23 team for the Olympic hockey squad. When they're playing test matches, it would now be perfectly feasible to play games in a different location each time, thus giving hockey fans around the country something to sink their teeth into. Regional Development Managers could be enlisted to entice people down, team sponsors could be used to run competitions to win match day tickets and local clubs engaged in order to bus youth team players in for the creation of a better atmosphere - something that the Spanish federation seem to have gotten the hang of, with some very noisy kids regularly seen and heard at their games in Valencia.

Media

More and more hockey matches are being shown on television recently. With the growth of the internet and development of broadband technologies, online streaming has been used to help show matches. Webcams have been used by a variety of clubs around the country to show what they are all about. However, improvements can always be made. Pre and post match analysis would be a positive step forward. Hockey pundits could be used to highlight what a team's strengths and weaknesses are for the average spectator, provide a background story to the players, as well as cover some basic talking points. During the coverage of the match, having at least one commentator is a useful method of painting a picture for those watching at home, as is the use of more than one camera angle. Having close up shots of the goal, or different lines of sight for short corner routines helps fans and students of the game to see what is happening at any given moment.

Producers should also be conscious of what the camera is showing the viewer. Looking out onto an empty field is not the most aesthetically pleasing sight in the world. Media operatives should ask themselves if it is possible to face the camera towards a main stand, or group of spectators. We want to see a glimpse of the atmosphere at the match, we want the feeling of being at the game itself. The showing of hockey online or television is about more than just showing the match. It's about telling the story of the contest, in a way that is accessible for the fans. It's about creating a spectacle.

Can There Be A Different Kind Of Fandom?

I have always been interested in fandom and support of a sports club, or a sportsperson. Culturally, we - and when I say 'we', I guess I mean the British sports fans, people that I know/socialise with, Western Civilisation in general - seem to be obsessed with fan culture and the following of and support of sports teams. Football, rugby and cricket clubs, professional athletes of individual pursuits such as golf, tennis and perhaps even darts. I'll stop short of carpet bowls. They all seem to have fans, supporters and followers. Whilst working in Mexico, I saw a tennis coach sporting a Roger Federer branded t-shirt. The distance and lack of any practical connection between an elite full time professional tennis player and a guy coaching in a posh sports club for amateur fee paying members in suburban Mexico City seems stretched, but there we go.

It's the same with football clubs. One thing that I have noticed wherever I have been around the world, is that there is an assorted collection of football shirts being worn by members of the local populace. Sometimes it is of a favourite team, perhaps with the name of a favoured player on the back, other times of a particular nation where that person hails from, or of a foreign club that a compatriot has gone to play for. These players are, by and large, hired mercenaries paid a wage that has given them a lifestyle that is vastly different from that of those who are wearing the shirts in support of these teams and players.

Some, if not many of these players care about the support of the fans, in the way that most people will enjoy applause. It offers an extrinsic valuation that is backed up with fame, fortune and cultural significance. This is in opposition to what fans - it would seem - actually want their favoured athletes to get out of their support; being a part of their community, adding something to what it means to be from that region, or group of people and representing what it means to be a part of that community in a positive manner.

On my bookshelf I have a copy of Pirates Punks and Politics; FC St. Pauli; Falling in Love with a Radical Football Club, by Nick Davidson. It is about an Englishman who fell back in love with following football, supporting a particular club and started to enjoy fan culture again after an extended period of absence from football stadia. What seemed different to me was that the club that promoted such change wasn't from his native Anglo-Saxon land, but that of Germany. FC St. Pauli is an established outfit from the German football leagues and seem to have become famous due to the political and social stances of the supporters and fan groups. This is a club where the majority of fans (although, there will always be differences of opinion in any large group of people) that take a strong stance against racism, fascism, sexism and homophobia. Davidson, the writer of this book, gave a history of the club, that ran alongside the contemporary history of its home nation and how it has grown within its home town. He described how the community of fans evolved from within a particular set of circumstances and how an ethos developed and found its voice within the terraces of a football club that is St. Pauli.

The general point of the book was that he felt more at home (in the context of his enjoyment of spectator sport) travelling from South East England to Hamburg in order to watch St. Pauli in the German 2nd division, than going to see Watford FC - the club that he had grown up supporting - in the English Premier Division. This, we are told, is partly due to his preference of how football fans are treated in Germany, but also how he felt that he fitted into a community of like minded people with the same view point as his. The writer of this book got involved in a community that he felt he could be a part of and contribute towards. It was based upon shared interests and beliefs, as well as a disillusionment at the lack of this in the branded, big business that has become the English version of football.

This strikes me as a different way of following sport. The fans do not necessarily need to support the club itself, due to regional or family affiliations, but the ethos and ideals surrounding the club. This may not be most convenient for some fans in terms of logistics - especially in the case of Nick Davidson, travelling across European borders, but in his opinion it can become more enjoyable. Additionally, it might also encourage PLC Football to pay more attention to fans, from a supply and demand point of view, forcing clubs to build community links in order to keep fans from disillusionment with the set-up and perhaps even bring new fans into the fold.

The Importance of Club Hockey

Hockey focuses far too much on the elite level of the international game. This scene is a fantastic aspect of the sport, with much entertainment to provide and many aspects to it for the rest of us to learn from. However, for far too many years, the national teams across the Home Nations and that of the combined Great Britain squads have dictated the resources of the game and hoarded them for their own needs and purposes. The centralised programme has taken players from all over Britain to the South-East of England, much to the detriment of the respective leagues.

The England/GB teams require the players to be within driving distance of the Bisham Abbey training base. The purpose of this has been to allow the players, the chosen few, to train together on a regular basis. This has created a platform for the national team to compete at a high level and is favoured by those who have been a part of the system. The England women's team have won the Commonwealth Games (Birmingham 2022) and the EuroHockey Championships (London 2015). In addition to this the Great British side won gold at the Olympic Games (Rio 2016). The men and women have also medaled consistently over the years at these major events and others, suggesting that the centralised programme does in fact work, or has done in the short term since its inception.

Although, there has been tangible recent benefits of holding all of the best players throughout the British Isles in a small region of England, I have my doubts about the long term benefits of this policy.

Recently, the Mancunian based team Bowdon Hightown Hockey Club were relegated from the English Women's Premier Division. They were the last team based north of the English Midlands to play in the top division. They've since been promoted again, but it shows the fragility of what is meant to be a national competition. In the men's game, only midlands based teams are competing as non southern clubs in the division. Brooklands Manchester University have recently been in the league, but have struggled to compete. There are a smattering of teams in the top women's and men's leagues based in Nottinghamshire and Leicestershire, but predominately clubs are from satellite towns of, or within London. East Grinstead, Surbiton, Wimbledon and Hampstead and Westminster seem to have been consistently near the top of the respective tables in recent years. Additionally, talented players from Scotland and Wales are encouraged to move to these areas, if they have ambitions to play in the Olympic Games.

Scotland and GB defender Amy Costello has recently moved back to England to play for Surbiton. Welsh goalkeeper, Toby Reynolds-Cotterill plays for Hampstead and Westminster, as does his talented compatriot and bustling forward Rupert Shipperly. Before going abroad to play in the Netherlands short corner specialist Jacob Draper was based here as well. The Wales women's midfielder, Sarah Jones, plays for Wimbledon. The recently capped GB international, Jen Eadie, was playing in the Scottish leagues only recently. She has since joined Jones in South London. They are joined in England by Scottish Ladies captain Sarah Robertson, well respected winger and Taysider Charlotte Watson, Fiona Burnet (also at Wimbledon) and midfielder Lee Morton in the men's set up, who's over at Old Georgians. I am only encouraging of these players as they look to get on in life. If you are a hockey player currently in, or approaching your prime and have ambitions to become an Olympian then this is a part of the game that you have to play.

Yes, the world is a smaller place, in this modern era. These players might have moved to London regardless of hockey opportunities, as the capital city tends to encourage talented people towards that part of the country anyway. The current British economy has a talent drain towards south-east. However, it would nice to have the option for the hard working clubs that invest time and effort to develop talented youth team players to reap the rewards for all of their hard work. The domestic side of the game is important for the development of hockey. It is how we all start out in the sport, it's where we predominately end up and it is an important method of community engagement. Here are some reasons as to why the national and international governing bodies should provide a bit more of a focus on the club scene...

Domestic Competitions

A strong league makes for a strong national team. If the players are regularly and constructively challenged on a weekly basis than this can only be good for the standard of the international matches that we see on the television. The centralised programme for Great Britain requires Scottish and Welsh players to travel south to England. Yes, by focusing all of the sports funding, resources and coaching into one place we can help these players to raise their standards, but what is the cost to the domestic leagues? By removing so many of the top players from their own communities then there will be an inevitable reduction in standards and learning opportunities for those left behind. Who have been forgotten? How many players have withered on the vine because of the current system's greed?

Stronger leagues across England, even in the north of the country, as well as Wales and Scotland, will see a larger pool of players develop for the Olympic squads. The men and the women will be able to compete with the best of the best more consistently and to a higher standard if they are being challenged in a more varied manner that strong league and cup tournaments can provide. This will not only benefit the international teams, but also the club sides in continental competitions. Wouldn't it be lovely if the British teams could perform better in the European Hockey League? The experiences gained from this elite club competition would greatly benefit those involved and increase their abilities and decision making processes. Improvements in the domestic championships will help to develop the top players available for selection.

It will also provide a place for tactics, strategy and style of play to be developed. A strong league is an environment for a culture to be grown and nurtured. A weak domestic competition will develop a poor culture, one with unwanted or unhelpful habits. A strong league and cup set up will encourage healthy habits, a better understanding of the game and a stronger culture within the sport that can be taken to the rest of the world. A national league and cup competition is not only a place to develop talent, but it is an environment to create an identity, a methodology and a style of play. It can provide a reference, a starting point, a mutual understanding. It can also provide nuance and some additional layers to the comprehension of hockey, with different clubs trying different things, or stretching each other in a variety of ways. This can only happen with a broad pool of players, who aren't taken down to the South-East of England, thus creating a very narrow field of play.

Development of the Grassroots and a Fan Culture

This conversation leads us on to the development of youth team players, the grassroots of the game. By keeping the talent local, this will provide role models for the younger players to look up to, admire and learn from through observation. These top players can also act as adverts for the game. Keeping them within their communities, or at least allowing them to periodically return, can show the uninitiated all of the positives and the values that come with hockey. It is a great game when played well, but if all of the professional athletes are in and around London, then how can we advertise it in the best possible manner, on a regular basis, in Manchester, Cardiff, Swansea, Edinburgh, or Glasgow? By ignoring the north of England, Wales and Scotland, we risk creating a smaller group of players and making hockey inaccessible to a vast array of talent.

Grassroots development is not confined to the education of youth team players. Domestic hockey leagues and cup competitions are also where the educators themselves start out. Coaches have to learn somewhere, they need to have some place to try out their ideas and theories. Tactics, stratagems and styles of play, as stated previously, can all be developed in the domestic arenas. The development of stronger league and cup competitions can also improve the standard of coaching, challenge old ideas, bring in some new ones and create some diversity of thought within the country and the sport. Coaches need a place to learn and to experiment. Doing this at the international stage is too late. It has to start with the clubs.

Improving the league and domestic scene can also help hockey to grow in the hearts and the minds of sports fans around a country. By providing some good sporting entertainment the game can begin to challenge larger, more mainstream sports, such as football, rugby and cricket. Spectators want a spectacle. Story tellers need a good story to tell. The clubs need the top players to stay locally in order to remain relevant within the sporting context of their communities. Quality breeds success and for clubs to engage with local fans they need to keep, or attract, the best players in the areas that they are based in.

A strong fan culture can have several benefits to the sport. The more people that are watching hockey, the more enticing it will be for potential sponsors. Visibility is what businesses want and if they can get that in hockey, then they will invest their money here, instead of elsewhere like netball, or other developing spectacles. Having fans coming through the gates and milling around the sides of the pitch can also increase revenues directly to the clubs themselves. Food kiosks, ticket stubs and replica kits can all be sources of income for teams and help them grow on their own terms.

Alternatives

There are alternatives to the current set up. Latterly in this book I have written about how hockey clubs can move towards professionalism, in the chapter Business and Sport. Briefly my ideas were based around the options of co-operative, fan based ownership and social enterprise/community interest companies (CIC). This would allow the clubs who already exist to grow and to develop and to help to professionalise the sport, out with the international scene, which is dependent on public funding tied to performance. It puts the control back into the hands of the clubs themselves. Fundamentally, the international players need to be released to their clubs on a more regular basis. A calendar and a schedule needs to be arranged, a compromise found between the international events and the domestic league and cup competitions. We must allow the top players, the famous faces, to play for their club sides throughout the season, especially in the finals and big games.

This can be done by keeping the format the same, or at least very similar to how things are currently set up in Britain. A strong domestic set up allows for a sense of connection between the lower levels of the game and the top. However, there are other options as well. The Oceanic countries have an interesting additional format. There's a regional league, that is different to the club system, which sits between that and the international team. In Australia, the Hockeyroos and the Kookaburras are both based in Perth, Western Australia (similar to the centralised system in the UK, however, it's a continent-sized country), but all the players are required to be registered with a team in their Hockey One League, which used to be a representative competition run for the local hockey associations. There are fewer teams than within the club scene, but it still gives local fans something to put their support behind and get their teeth into.

The British did something similar a few years ago, with the GB Super League. This was a competition that was used as a talent showcase between 2007 and 2012. It had six teams within it, three from England (Wessex Leopards, Saxon Tigers and Pennine Pumas), two from Scotland (Caledonian Cougars and Highland Jaguars) and one from Wales (Celtic Panthers). The names are a bit naff and it didn't quite take off at the first time of trying, but it could be something worth continuing with as a compromise. A revamp of this idea could allow us to keep some sort of domestic set up, where players can go back to the communities to which they feel some kind of connection.

Played over a shortened period of time, a reduced season could be tailored to fit in with other commitments and a busy schedule. In order to increase fan interest, we would need some sort of sense of competition, to develop an edge that comes with results driven consequences, therefore a second and maybe even a third tier would be necessary. More teams could be developed that included international youth team players from the GB Elite Development Programme, as well as giving the chance to the better club players in order to show what they can do. This, combined with the emergence of a moveable astroturf pitch, we could create a spectacle that can be set up in appropriate stadiums and locations around the country and in each specific region. It's something to think about at the very least...

The Importance of Indoor Hockey

The sport of hockey has three variations. The more traditional 11-a-side game is what we see at the Olympic Games and in the televised matches that are broadcast on the pay-per-view channels. There's a new version that seems to be favoured by International Governing Body, the FIH, which is Hockey 5's. This code has had its criticisms, in terms of the aesthetic qualities that comes from having only four outfield players, safety concerns around being able to shoot from outside the circle and the focus on this short hand variation of the sport, when there is already another one firmly established across the world and worthy of celebration.

Indoor hockey is a six-a-side alternative to the larger outdoor game. It is a variant developed in Germany during the 1950's and quickly spread to other countries, with national teams such as Belgium, Austria and the Netherlands becoming particularly strong in the international competitions. However, it isn't just Central European teams that have done well in indoor hockey. Former Soviet states and Baltic countries have proven themselves worthy of merit. Belarus, Ukraine, Poland, Russia and the Czech Republic are all placed well within the FIH World Rankings. At the point of writing, the Iranian men's team are also ranked third in this list, well above their outdoor rankings. This seems to be a common thread that runs through the top teams in the world and why we see some variation in the national sides that compete for honours. Similarly for club teams, although the European competitions have been dominated by the Germans; indoor hockey has provided opportunities for sides hailing from national federations that are traditionally smaller in the outdoor scene, the chance to compete and medal at a high level.

It has also provided the chance for players to make a name for themselves, even become specialists. There are those who have found success in both indoor and outdoor codes of hockey, sometimes even creating a name for themselves in the 6-a-side version. Michael Körper springs to mind as one of the more well known figures in the Austrian men's side. His national team is far more competitive in the indoor competitions than the outdoor events, thus helping him to achieve greater recognition. Other players are able to find success across the board, with greater opportunities in the different tournaments. Lisa Altenburg, for example, has won medals in both indoor and outdoor tournaments, including gold at the 2018 Indoor World Cup and a bronze at the 2016 Olympic Games.

In Britain we have several players and clubs who do well at indoor hockey. The English Super 6's tournament is the pre-eminent indoor event in the country. Surbiton, Wimbledon and East Grinstead tend to dominate the Premier Divisions across both the men's and women's championships. Simon Faulkner and Richard Lane have both made good careers for themselves playing the six-a-side version of the game at East Grinstead, with even Czech internationals Filip Neusser (a world renowned goalkeeper) and Katerina Lacina, both having turned out recently for this club, in the South-East of England. However, Bowdon Hightown make a strong showing in the women's setup, with GB Olympic medalists Sam Quek, Sally Walton and Tina Cullen involved there. Additionally, Buckingham Ladies won their first national title in 2020, with the help of coach Zak Jones.

There have been several success stories across Scotland as well. Dundee Wanderers have traditionally had a very strong side. They have produced several international standard players, including former outdoor co-captain Becky Bruce (née Ward), Emily Dark of the GB EDP and Charlotte Watson who has played a few games for Great Britain. Even from the men's side, they have also given starts to local lads Ross and Niall Stott. Ross, who has played over 120 times for Scotland including at the 2010 and 2014 Commonwealth Games, while his brother played for GB at the Olympic Games. One of Dundee's main rivals is Clydesdale Western, with the women's teams meeting regularly in the Grande Finale of the Scottish Indoor Championships.

Inverleith Hockey Club also tends to do quite well, having won the National Championships and representing their country at continental competitions on more than one occasion, they regularly give opportunities for players to develop. Derek Salmond, who is the club's men's player of the decade and has played for Scotland at the Commonwealth Games, still turns out for the indoor side. Greg Mackenzie is a specialist indoor goalkeeper for Inverleith, and has been capped at international level for his country.

Furthermore, in terms of Scottish goalkeeping, both the senior men's and women's outdoor goalkeepers have had successful careers in indoor hockey, having won Bundesliga titles, whilst playing over in Germany. Amy Gibson was a well respected goalie, who has recently returned to the UK and subsequently retired after having spent several years at Der Club An Der Alster. Tommy Alexander is still out there, playing to a high level, currently with the same club, previously having turned out for UHC Hamburg. These experiences can only benefit their respective national teams.

This variation obviously has many benefits that allows for diversity in participation and success. We, the stakeholders of the sport, already have a short hand for the sport that provides the advertised benefits of Hockey 5's. This begs the question of what makes indoor hockey special? What exactly is the uniqueness of this game that makes it such a good spectacle? Let's explore a few details together...

Set Up of Indoor Hockey

There are a few differences in the rules of indoor hockey compared to the outdoor game. Firstly, the pitch is smaller, the court being 18 to 22 metres wides, by 36 to 44 metres long, with the shooting circle measured 9 metres out from each goal post. Teams consist of six players, including a goalkeeper, with a maximum of 12 in the squad with rolling substitutes. The FIH standard time for games is 20 minutes in each half. In the German leagues they play 30 minutes each way, with the opportunities for time outs to be called for team talks.

Additionally, there's a unique playing style to the game. Players are unable to strike, or hit the ball, only being allowed to push or deflect it. The only time that the ball is allowed to be lifted is when a shot on goal is attempted. This provides an increase in difficulty levels for indoor hockey. These conditions on the players, when combined with the smaller pitch, mean that individual skill and anticipation, as well as team work and movement off the ball is essential in order to succeed. An over reliance on physical attributes, such as speed and power over longer distances are ineffective. Players are encouraged to play the game, instead of using physical force.

This has training benefits. If players are able to take the technical skills and decision making experiences that they have gained from indoor hockey into the outdoor game then this can create a better spectacle for televised events such as the Olympic Games. The two variations, although mutually exclusive, can help each other in terms of development of players, teams and media coverage.

Spectacle of Indoor Hockey

The way that indoor hockey has been set up has allowed for a fast, exciting and entertaining spectacle that, in my opinion, is vastly superior to Hockey 5's. By having six players on the pitch, instead of the five in the newer version, allows for a better aesthetic. The additional player allows for more passing moves to be made, with give and goes available all over the court and attacking overloads being encouraged. The reduction of this by one inadvertently encourages the more physical traits associated with the 11-a-side code, such as sprinting past an opponent and whacking the ball as hard as you can. Six players on a team makes for a better passing game.

The shorter game times can also have a positive effect on the consumption of the sport, from a fans point of view. With the standard 40 minute matches, more fixtures can be played in a day and give the perception of better value for money with regards a ticket stub. Spectators can turn up at a venue and take in a variety of different teams, playing styles and famous faces, all within one afternoon. The appeal of this can be easily marketed to create additional revenue streams for clubs, national governing bodies and federations. It can also act as a method of inspiration for future generations of players. The watching of skilful players at a high tempo can get spectators hooked and kept in the game. Indoor hockey is an advert for the wider sports fans to get involved…

Practicalities of Indoor Hockey

There are a variety of practical ways in which running and organising an indoor hockey team is cheaper, easier and more accessible. As mentioned earlier, the playing area for the game is a lot smaller than the 11-a-side outdoor code and potentially more cost effective. It is currently played in sports halls which can be found in towns and cities across the length and breadth of Britain, in leisure centres and community hubs. This would be a fantastic place to go to in order to escape the climatic experiences in England, Scotland, or Wales, especially during the winter months. There's also no reason why the sport can't be played outdoors, under the same rules and regulations, if that's what clubs want to do.

The obvious benefit of indoor hockey is that team managers can work with fewer players, thus needing a smaller pool of talent. If a club is based in a smaller hockey community, or a national team has fewer registered players than their neighbours than the six-a-side game could be the answer to being competitively viable. This has worked for national sides such as Austria, Iran and Poland. It could also work well for Ireland, Scotland and Wales, who all have a history of producing talented players in small waves. By having the opportunity to put out teams with smaller squad sizes, these national sides will be able to compete at a higher level on a more consistent basis. If the league structure is given time, space and funding in order to flourish then this will have a positive effect on the international teams, improving the technical skill sets and decision making processes of those involved, as well as their chances for success. Indoor hockey has the potential to raise the standard of play within any given hockey playing country.

Business and Sport

The Corinthian Spirit still has prevalence in the UK. This is the ideal to play sport for the love of the game, to be the best at something, without even trying – the Good Amateur. Terms such as 'Journeyman' and 'Mercenary' are common within the mass football/sports mass media, which is full of connotations and fables to do with athletes and players participating out of some sense of purity.

Playing for the love of the game is an indirect slander about professionalism and the act of making a living from sport, training hard to become better at their job and treating his or her chosen game in the same way that a manual labourer would treat his or her employment. The Corinthian Footballers – an amateur organisation of upper class 'Gentlemen' – were fantastic in their day. At one point they provided an entire starting eleven for an England match. As professionalism entered English football, the Corinthians even took strong results in friendlies and test matches against championship and cup winning clubs. This success was based upon a strong sporting background at school and university level, athleticism and the inefficiencies (I suspect) from other teams.

As professional clubs started to become stronger and figured out what worked (and what didn't) the Corinthians started to see a decline in their powers.

This is an early, if not the first example, of professionalism overtaking top-drawer amateurs. There has been a steady turning of the tide ever since. Now, if a person wants to get to the top level of many of the mainstream sports, if he or she wants to get to the Olympics, then they need to either be a professional, or have a funding scheme (either through public or private investment), which allows a focusing on training and competition. Through treating sports participation and athleticism as a job and approaching it as such, the contracted participant becomes a better athlete and thus the standards of play have improved dramatically.

Men's football got on board with professionalism and business early doors. Public Limited Companies (PLC's) were created, or were used to take over football clubs. The board members and directors were then able to make some money for the first time, turning their initial investments into significant financial returns (which was frowned upon previously) and to also re-invest money back into the club itself. This made the football clubs more profitable and business like in ethos and the move towards the entertainment industry had begun.

This was unheard of at the time. Up until the 1960s and 1970s football clubs were meant to be hobbies for the local 'Billy Big Bucks' businessmen to lose money, gain prestige and bolster their egos. This turn to PLC's helped to move the game forward, in only a few years. Big business helped to improve stadium design (at the behest of the British Court system), created a huge number of new jobs in an ever growing section of the sports industry and used marketing to open the game to a wider new audience. Players (often from the working classes) found their earning potential increase, thus attracting higher quality players over to the English leagues. As the standards rose British football became all the more enjoyable – a better spectacle, a stronger product.

Along the way, something has been lost. As somebody who has grown up in a generation of sports fans that was sold on football through the glitz and the glamour of the English Premier League, I'm not sure exactly what it is, but I'm missing something. The older generations talk and write about a sense of community, a sense of belonging with a group of people that you saw on a regular basis and had a passion for a game similar to your own. I was somebody who couldn't afford to attend football games on a regular basis, having been priced out of games, I missed out on this. I grew up in London, where the club I followed, a Spurs side that was largely inferior to previous or later incarnations, were charging the same amount as it cost to watch the England national team. This sense of supporting a football club has always seemed foreign to me. It does occur to me that I had chosen to follow the results of a bunch of hired hands and mercenaries. I think that the ethos of support that football fans have been traditionally brought up to believe in and to partake in is similar to what I got when I started playing amateur level hockey for small clubs. I desire to be a part of something that can grow and that, along with others, I can call my own – I can say that I was a part of the success and failure of something that I helped to create.

Women's football poses an interesting development within the sport of football. In England, it has recently turned professional. The Women's Super League (WSL) has two divisions with a mix of full and part time players at clubs, with central contracts available for the England international players. But the players themselves still seem accessible to those who attend matches. Many of the professional athletes can still remember the dark days before the WSL, when they were struggling to get recognition, decent pay and injury rehabilitation. Most of them still have to deal with sexism and misogyny on a regular basis. Now the women have the potential to become nationally and internationally recognisable stars and to make a good living. A few years ago Manchester United FC drew criticism for not fielding a senior women's team. Many of the other men's Premier League clubs had provided greater opportunities for their female players, whilst the Mancunian reds were comparatively slower to join the party, finally entering the WSL second division in 2018. A year or so before this, Rachel Brown-Finnis, an ex-England international goalkeeper, wrote an article for BBC Sport criticising the apparent lack of eagerness. She said that the club has a duty to women and girls in sport. This is actually untrue, if only in terms of practicality if not sentiment, and is a failing of this type of business in sport. Manchester United is no longer a football club that purely exists for its local community, if that's what it was in its beginning. It is a football club that is run by a PLC, as a business, and is fundamentally a profit making enterprise. This is perhaps not suited for an entity that is culturally, as well as socially, expected to be for its supporter base and used by the community that it is based in.

This begs the question that I would ask of minority and developing sports. If they want to professionalise themselves, how would they want to do it? Do they want to copy the model put forward by English men's football, or would they fancy an alternative?

Handball, netball and basketball in the UK might all find the templates listed below useful, but as a hockey coach, I particularly had this sport in mind. Hockey, in Britain and much of the world, is still broadly speaking an amateur sport. The majority of club players, even at the top level pay to play for their clubs. There are alternative ways to organise a hockey club, or even other types of sports clubs;

1. Co-operative. Fan based ownership.
2. Social Enterprise/Community Interest Company (CIC). All profits are reinvested back into the local community that the company is based within

Co-operative run, fan owned clubs have started to crop up in the football industry. Supporter based groups have been buying into and/or taking over their local clubs all over the United Kingdom, as well as other countries. In the men's game Brentford FC (who promoted to the Premier League in 2021), Wycombe Wanderers FC, Exeter City FC, AFC Wimbledon, FC United of Manchester have all shown that the community can run clubs for the community basis. Depending on how much control over the club that the fans have, this can allow the supporters to have varying degrees of control.

FC United of Manchester and AFC Wimbledon were both set up in protest after what the larger local club had done in terms of big business. They have been largely acclaimed as putting a friendly face back on the game of football in England. Football fans no longer have to put up with large co-corporations when engaging with their local football club. They can take back control.

Community Interest Companies (CICs) are businesses that look to make money, but all of the profits are re-invested into the communities that they are based in and serve. CICs have been described as businesses with a conscience. Employees are paid a salary and can be paid a competitive wage, but no money is given to shareholders, because there aren't any shareholders, therefore the ethos of the company can be that of what is best for the local area, the staff, the relevant industry. CICs can conduct positive work practices, without worrying about pleasing profit driven shareholders.

This is something that I don't believe has been introduced into sports business at the top end. I am not aware of any sports club that is set up in this manner. It is run at the behest of the local community and even makes money for that community, but is run like a business. I would highly recommended these concepts for hockey and other minority sports. In terms of hockey, a CIC would be set up in a very similar method to how many of the existing amateur clubs are already being organised. They need a chairperson (or a president), a secretary, and a treasurer to keep accurate financial records. It means that businesses can get involved, professionalism can improve the standard of the organisation and the sport itself, without forgetting about its roots.

Hockey Rivalries

Sport is, from its conception, competitive. It is normal for teams and clubs to develop a sense of combativeness, either jovial or otherwise, between each other. Hockey is no different to any other code, game, or activity that is out there. There are the rivalries that are based upon geography, resentment, jealousy, or bad blood from coming up against each other in the same tournaments. However, unlike other sports such as football, rugby and cricket, hockey fans are broadly unaware of what has been going on, unless they have been directly involved. So, let's have a look at some of the rivalries that developed within the sport of hockey…

Argentina

The Torneo Metropolitano de Hockey is the preeminent hockey tournament in the Buenos Aires Province of Argentina. Buenos Aires is the dominant hockey playing region of the leading hockey country in the Pan American region. So, it could be said that this is an important domestic hockey competition. Out of this has sprung a rivalry based upon not only a desire for dominance, but also locality, between Ciudad and GEBA.

Club Ciudad de Buenos Aires are a sports and social club, based in the Núñez district of the Argentine capital city. Originally founded in 1920, they put on a variety of different sports including basketball, football and rugby. However, hockey is the largest sport at the club and they have found a broad amount of success between their men's and women's teams, who both play in the Primera División of the Metropolitano. The men have won the league on 15 occasions, the joint second amount of times in the tournament's history, with the women winning five titles.

Gimnasia y Esgrima de Buenos Aires, more commonly known as GEBA, are another multi sports club based in Buenos Aires. Set up in 1880, they are one of the oldest sports clubs in Argentina, who put on around 30 different activities on any given season. They are well known, like their cross city rivals Ciudad, for basketball, football and rugby, but have also had a lot of success in hockey, with some famous players having turned out for them. Former Argentinian men's team player Patricio Cammareri has played for them in the past, however, it is the amount of top female players that have worn the shirt that is notable. Silvina D'Elia, and Florencia Habif have both played for GEBA and found success with Las Leonas. One player in particular stands out more than any other in Argentine hockey. Two time World Champion and four time Olympic Medalist, Luciana Aymar (the Maradona of field hockey) turned out for the club between 2008 and 2011. GEBA have won the women's Metropolitano title nine times.

The Ciudad versus GEBA match is not only a local derby, but one of ambition. Elite clubs always want to win titles and there is a tendency to dislike anybody who gets in their way. This can only be heightened by the clubs being so close to each other, within Buenos Aires. As they are also both multi-sports clubs, there may well be added rivalries that derive from their match ups elsewhere.

Scotland

Hockey in Scotland has, at various times, been dominated by the teams in the two largest cities in the country. Edinburgh, next to the Firth of Forth in the East, is the political and economic capital, with an approximate population of 550,000. The Scottish Parliament is based here, as is the former seat of power for the Scottish monarchy, Holyrood Palace. The 1970 and 1986 Commonwealth Games were held in the city, with several of the sports venues still remaining around town. Edinburgh has a strong literary history, with Robert Louis Stevenson's book, The Strange Case of Dr. Jekyll and Mr. Hyde based upon the life of the rather naughty Edinburgher, Deacon William Brodie. Other writers hail from the town; J.K. Rowling wrote the first Harry Potter novel in a cafe here and

Irvine Welsh wrote Trainspotting, as well as other novels, based around the Leith area. Additionally, film star Sean Connery was a local lad.

Glasgow, on the West Coast, has a population of around 1.6 million people. It has benefited largely from industrial development, specifically around the shipyards. It also has a thriving music and arts scene. Bands such as Simple Minds, Del Amitri, Texas and Franz Ferdinand are all Glaswegian. Other well known sons include actors Peter Capaldi and James McAvoy and musician Stevie Young, who's the guitarist for AC/DC. Comedian Billy Connelly in fact worked as a welder in the Glaswegian shipyards. Football manager Sir Alex Ferguson is also from the city, having played for Rangers in the 1960's.

Most of the big Scottish hockey clubs come from these two cities. In the women's game, Edinburgh University have had a lot of recent success, in both the league and the cup competitions. However, more recently Watsonians have become a bit stronger, having won the league title in 2022 and 2023. Being that they are both based in the same town, we have local pride as well as competitive rivalry, at stake here. Staying in Edinburgh there are a variety of clubs to look at. Inverleith have over a 100 year history and currently have both men and women in the Scottish Premiership and a very good indoor side. The Grange is one of the biggest hockey clubs in the country for men and women. They often compete at the highest level, regularly qualifying for the European Hockey League. Over the years they have rutted against West Coast clubs Kelburne and Western Wildcats. These are the two biggest clubs to have come out of Glasgow and in recent years have gone head to head with their East Coast rivals for league and cup titles. Former Scottish Ladies captain Kareena 'Kaz' Cuthbert recently coached Western Wildcats Ladies to the Scottish title.

Outside of the Central Belt (the strip of Scotland between Edinburgh and Glasgow), we have the two biggest clubs from the region of Tayside. Grove Menzieshill and Dundee Wanderers both have proud histories. Grove Menzieshill have represented Scotland in European competitions a dozen times in the past decade. In 2016 they received the honour of European Club of the Year, from the European Hockey Federation. Dundee Wanderers take their name from the town that both sides are based in. They have a variety of outdoor national titles across their men's and women's teams. However, they are well known for their success within the indoor code of hockey. They won the women's Scottish Indoor title in 2009 and took the Men's Cup in 1998. The men's team also took home the Indoor European B Division in 1991. Wanderers have produced several top international players. In the current women's GB and Scotland squads Charlotte Watson has only recently left Scotland to take up her contract as a part of the centralised programme. Former Scotland ladies captain Becky Bruce (née Ward), hails from Tayside and came through at Wanderers.

Similarly, the Stott brothers started out at Dundee Wanderers. Niall Stott went on to play for Great Britain at the Athens 2004 Olympic Games. Ross Stott has also had a successful career, winning titles across Britain, playing for both Grove Menzieshill and Dundee Wanderers. He was a part of the Scotland squad at the 2010 and 2014 Commonwealth Games. As somebody who has crossed the Tayside divide, he had this to say about the fixture,

"The Dundee derby was always a physical game, a lot of chat, off the ball incidents. Tackles were 100%. The hockey wasn't always that good but I think with my generation the rivalry kind of died down a bit as we all played age groups with each other and where friends, for instance Gav Byers is one of my good mates. In the 1990s and early 2000s probs when it [the rivalry] was at its highest, especially indoor. Having played on both sides I would say that it was Wanderers that held the rivalry more, I got some chat from the fans and players when I played against them for Menziehill. Not sure what it's like these days but hockey needs these rivalries in my opinion."
(Ross Stott, December 2022)

International

There are many international derbies around the world. Any match between the British Home Nations of England, Scotland and Wales is always seen as a bit of a ding dong affair. Additionally, with Ireland just next door, there is a local rivalry there as well. The first ever international hockey fixture was between Ireland and Wales (men) in Rhyl in 1895, with the Irish running out winners with three goals to nil. England's men played their first ever game in the same year, against the Emerald Isle, at Richmond, which the Anglo-Saxons won five nil. It wasn't until a year later, in 1896, before the first ever women's international was played. Again this was between England and Ireland, but this time in Dublin with the home side winning two nil.

This rivalry has continued over the preceding years. More recently, a particular match stands out between England and Ireland. It happened at the 2015 EuroHockey Championships, held in London. Hockey Ireland governs hockey across both Northern Ireland and the Republic to the South. In the 2000's a few players from around the Belfast area decided that they no longer wanted to play for Ireland, but for Great Britain instead. This meant that they had to choose one of the three aforementioned home nations and selected to play for England. The Bronze Medal Match of the EuroHockey Championships saw Ireland in fact beat

England on their home pitch. It was made all the more notable as Mark Gleghorne (one of the players who moved across) lost the match to his younger brother Paul, who had elected to stay with his national team of birth.

The Netherlands and Germany is considered a classical international matchup. The two countries share a border and the Dutch were occupied by the Germans during the Second World War. The rivalry also crosses over into other sports, such as football. However, these two nations are also two very strong hockey playing nations in both the indoor and outdoor codes, and have had much success over the years. Unfortunately, these two teams have only met twice on the Olympic Games Finals, once in the men's tournament and once in the women's. The Germans came out on top on both occasions. In London 2012 the German men's team (Honamas) beat the Dutch by one goal to nil. Die Danas struck gold in Athens 2004, beating the Netherlands two one. The Dutch have faired much better in the Women's World Cup, winning nine times, two of those occasions they did so by beating West Germany in the Gold Medal Match.

Similarly, India and Pakistan have a national sporting rivalry that has lasted for many years. It stems from the partitioning of Pakistan from India in 1947. India won the men's Olympic hockey tournament for six tournaments in a row. The record breaking run of titles was only stopped by their northern neighbours in Rome, 1960. In fact this fixture was the Olympic Men's Hockey Final for three Olympiads in a row; Melbourne 1956, India 1-0 Pakistan; Rome 1960 Pakistan 1-0 India; Tokyo 1964, India 1-0 Pakistan.

In terms of continental success, Pakistan come out on top, statistically speaking. The men's team have won the Asian Games a record eight times, more than any side from the men's or women's games. Starting in 1958, there has been 16 hockey tournaments at this multi-sports event. Only twice have India, or Pakistan not featured in the Grande Finale, the first time of which wasn't until 2006, which was contested between South Korea and China (Pakistan came third). Nine of the Finals have been between the two rivals. Seven of Pakistans eight gold medals have come by beating India into second place, whilst India have only won the competition three times, beating their neighbours on two occasions in 1966 and 2014.

The Pakistanis have won the Men's World Cup four times since its inception in 1971, more times than anybody else. Compared to India's one world title, they have the upper hand in this respect. However, the solitary time that India have won the World Cup was also the only time that we have seen the two teams compete in the final game of the competition. India won this match by two goals to one.

Unfortunately, this rivalry at the elite level has only been borne out at in the men's game, as the Pakistani women haven't been able to compete at the same level as the Indians. These days it's generally considered that India have the stronger hockey programme, as their respective teams are consistently competing at a higher standard to that of their rivals. The Indian men's side took the bronze medal at the 2024 Paris Olympics, with the women finishing fourth in Tokyo.

In the late 1990s and early 2000s an unlikely rivalry emerged between Asian stalwarts Malaysia and Canada, a North American side better known for the sort of hockey played on ice. It started at a 1996 Olympic Games qualifying event in Barcelona. In the final game of the round robin group matches, India (who had already secured their place at the tournament) faced Malaysia. If the Indians won it, then the Canadians would qualify for the Olympic Games. However, the game ended in a draw. Surprisingly for two traditionally attacking teams, both sides only racked up one shot apiece and Malaysia went through instead. The Canadians were outraged. Sensing some sort of collaboration, they made allegations along those lines. However, nothing was proved, but the incident sparked years of animosity.

In recent times, The Belgian and Australian men's teams have been fighting for the top spot in world hockey over the last few years. They have both alternatively been ranked number one in the FIH World Rankings at one point or another in the last few years, with both making the Grande Finale of the Tokyo 2020(21) Olympic hockey tournament. Belgium came out on top of this fixture, but only after a penalty shootout. Unfortunately this fixture wasn't seen at the 2023 Men's World Cup, as both teams managed to avoid each other, with the Australians missing out on the medals, finally finishing in fourth place and the Belgians losing out to Germany in the Grande Finale.

Chapter Six - Coaching

What Makes a Good Coach?

What makes a good coach? What makes a top-notch manager, these days? What differentiates a first-rate coach or manager, from a those in days gone by, if anything does at all?

Previously, I read a book called 'Hockey, a Philosophical Game', by Andreu Enrich. Here he writes about how the quest for control destroys the sports coach, because one cannot control every aspect of an ever changing and evolving hubbub of activity that is a competitive match, or team environment. Instead he emphasises that coaches should attempt to influence situations and thus have a much healthier and constructive approach to the role. Enrich describes the ability to influence a player, team, or situation as being a more long-term method for success than control, not only to reduce stress and anxiety, but to improve relationships amongst others and improve outcomes.

This got me thinking about some of the coaches and mangers that I grew up admiring in the world of sports. These were straight talking men, from no nonsense backgrounds, whose personal identity was wrapped up in how they put their own will and perspective onto a group of players. A sports coach was expected to have authority over his (and at the time it was almost certainly a man in charge) dominion. Any kind of sway from this standard would be a check against the manager's self image and sense of doing the job properly. It would have a negative impact on his ego. In football, Sir Alex Ferguson and Brian Clough were both known to work with a firm hand. Sir Alex was once quoted by the Guardian as saying,

"You can't ever lose control – not when you are dealing with 30 top professionals who are all millionaires. If they misbehave, we fine them, but we keep it indoors. And if anyone steps out of my control, that's them dead."

Famously, when Brian Clough was asked what happens when one of his players might come to him with a critique of his management, his response was,

"Well, I ask him, which way he thinks it should be done. We get down to it and then we talk about it for twenty minutes and then we decide I was right."

Does this method of coaching work today? Do players respond to this sort of management these days, in the way they did in the 1970s, '80s and '90s…?

This attitude did seem to work, as both of these football managers won numerous trophies, including English league titles, and more than one European Cup each. Alex Ferguson even took his national team of Scotland to the 1986 World Cup. A tournament that neither Cloughie nor Fergie saw as players. This self deterministic mindset helped them both achieve success as managers in their own right, as well as having given opportunities to have good careers to many players who played under them. Both coaches, however, fell out with those who challenged them, having negative impacts on those who the managers had the opportunity to guide and improve. Swings and roundabouts, some might say. People aren't always going to get along. Some players will want different things to and from their bosses and vice versa. Sport is, or at the very least has been, a high octane work environment where people habitually think in black and white and struggle with grey areas that can be argued in either direction.

However, as we move further into the twentieth century and workplace standards improve should we expect sports to follow this professional enlightenment? The football fans reading this might remember that the English FA were recently proven (in a legal sense) to have used awfully poor work place practices when dealing with several complaints from players. It was based around claims of racism and then ostracism. This was the case involving Eniola Aluko, and other cases including Drew Spence, Anita Asante and Lianne Sanderson (all of whom were English players of African, and/or Caribbean heritage) being pushed aside by Mark Sampson, after their assertion against his authority due to his inappropriate behaviour towards them. The FA looked to blame everybody apart from themselves and Mark Sampson, before they were successfully legally challenged. I put it to the reader that these players probably wouldn't have gotten the result and latterly the apologies that they did get, in decades gone past and I still think that they have been given a bum deal (my personal opinion, based on my reading of things so far). The potential for careers to be cut short, tabloid speculation and psychological stress induced by a variety of social factors can give those in positions lacking authority a number of hurdles to clear before receiving fair treatment.

The question that I am posing here is should sports coaches and managers be less autocratic, whilst still looking to influence individuals and broader groups. What does the modern coach look like? How much control should be given to one person, when dealing with the all too short careers of athletes? How much should we be empowering the players themselves and how does this work within a group dynamic when people within the same team want to go in different directions?

Let's start by looking at the meaning of the words that we are talking about. If we take the Oxford Dictionary and Thesaurus that my mother gave me upon starting secondary school we can get a clearer idea of what we mean.

Control
Power to give orders or restrain
Means of restraining or regulating
Standard of comparison for checking results of an experiment

Influence
Effect a person or thing has on another
Moral power, ascendancy
Person or thing with this

Empower
Authorise, enable

These definitions are important when reflecting on how to improve an individual athlete, or a group of players and a team in general. Now, before I give my personal opinion, I should probably state that my coaching career has predominately focused on developmental youth teams. When I have coached adult sides, it has been reserve teams and/or social groups. They haven't been at the elite level of competition. However, I do feel that a good coach should be focused on the empowerment of the players on the pitch, through his or her experience, influence and guidance.

This is not to say that control has no place at all in the tool box of a sports coach. Control can be used to get a rogue player back on track. If an individual is making decisions that are detrimental to the wider group then they might need a firm nudge in a healthier or more productive direction. It can also be used in the short term, before trust is earned on both sides of a relationship, although this has its pitfalls and variables. A controlled test or experiment can also produce objective results over the course of a season that can help guide the staff, administrators and the players towards better learning outcomes. Control of style of play, tactics and strategy will probably have a better impact on results, than a committee who all pull in different directions.

The actual coaching of a player or a team should be far more of an exercise in empowerment. Once the match, game or event starts, then there is very little that a coach can do. Yes, there are adaptations that can be made, especially in invasion sports, such as hockey, football and rugby, for example. However, most of the coaching and management is done in preparation on the training field and video analysis rooms. Players should be helped to solve problems for themselves. This can be done, technically (can you beat the defender), tactically (how can we work together to get past a defensive block), or psychologically (I think I can, I know I can…). All of these things come under the gentler and more enriching approach of an influential coach, rather than a controlling one. Although it might take longer, the building of relationships is essential here, but as Andreu Enrich tells us, it can produce better, healthier results.

Coaching Opinion; The Benefits of Small Sided Games

Over the past few of seasons, I have been coaching in a variety of roles at Inverleith Hockey Club, based in the Scottish capital city Edinburgh. As a youth hockey coach, I have been tasked with helping out with the development of the less experienced players here. I'm always thinking about ways in which to engage, encourage and provide learning opportunities to the children and young people in my groups and teams. There are many different ideas for how to go about things, however, I do have some preferences.

Small sided games are a useful method to recreate the situations of a competitive match in a training context. One versus one, two versus two, three versus three are all team sizes that I use on a regular basis. On a larger scale, indoor hockey is a short hand version of the sport with six players on either side, which has tactical and technical benefits for those who play both indoor and outdoor codes. Those who come back from the smaller game after Christmas, often talk about increased abilities and mental sharpness. This could be because the rules and regulations associated with indoor hockey help to promote passing and movement attributes within a team setting.

When a coach uses small sided games during training, there are a variety of benefits for the players. A technical director that I used to work for talked about random repetition a lot. The exposure to primary, secondary and tertiary learning outcomes, happen on a regular basis. Players will be able to use different types of technique and tactical decision making processes when passing, shooting, tackling, attacking and defending, in a variety of different positions, angles and situations. Additionally, I often change the shape of the pitch, between rectangles that are longer than they are wide, wider than they are long, as well as squares. Other conditions include moving targets from the right, to the left and then to the centre of the base line, having more than one target to aim for, as well as giving bonus points for moving the ball through certain targets, winning the ball in specified areas and creating overloads in highlighted positions on the pitch (often splitting the playing area into sections, for example thirds). All of these methods are designed to encourage certain behaviours and choices through visual means and positive reinforcement.

The benefits of all of this is that the players are given the opportunity to make mistakes, realise what they are and then to have the chance to correct them again and again and again, as often as possible. When playing in smaller teams, or even in a one versus one situation, the chances are increased that the player will find him, or herself, in the desired situation to improve and to find success regularly during the training session.

Random repetition is about providing players a match like situation, linked to the primary learning objective, often and regularly, but in an ever changing context. Therefore, if the team is working on passing, the ball carrier has to decide whether to move the ball softly, or firmly, evade the defender in the initial instance, or drive into space first, or even in which way to move the ball, therefore changing the angle of the stick and feet. I would recommend that all coaches include small sided games in their session plans.

Iconic Hockey Coaches

It's time to celebrate the personalities in hockey. There is a long list of brilliant people who have coached within the game and provided us with plenty of entertainment over the years. Coaches direct the tactics and strategy of a team. They pick the players, as well as taking the lead in setting the culture and ethos of a squad. There is a wide ranging array of responsibilities within a coach's or manager's remit, allowing him or her to have a variety of ways to move things forward.

In this list of iconic hockey coaches, I have used a set of criteria that includes success, status and innovation to a certain extent, but also the individual's public persona. I've gone for putting the names down in alphabetical order, instead of any other specific arrangement. People will inevitably disagree with me in some shape, or form, but I've predominately gone for those who I find interesting, made me smile and/or have helped me to enjoy hockey a little bit more. There are six coaches on this list, as six is the magic number in hockey…

Alyson Annan

Hailing from Australia, she was a very successful player in her own right. In 2003 she hung up her stick and became a coach within the Dutch league, taking on HC Klein Zwitserland, then Amsterdamsche Hockey and Bandy Club. Having assisted Marc Lammers with the Dutch National Team in 2004, Annan became the head coach of her adoptive nation in 2015. Here she went on to take her women's side to two Olympic finals, winning in Tokyo 2020, as well as lifting the 2018 World Cup.

By the time the 2022 World Cup had come around, she had taken on a new project, with the Chinese women's team and helping them to play some good hockey along the way. In 2023 China won the continental championships, the Asian Games, which allowed for direct qualification to the 2024 Paris Olympic Games. It was here that Alyson coached her side to the silver medal, getting past her home nation Australia in the quarter-finals and then forcing her former Dutch side to a penalty shootout in the grande finale. This was an unexpected performance for her side, showing the impact that good coaching and tactical intelligence can have on a group keen to learn. In 2013 Annan was inducted into the Sport Australia Hall of Fame.

Max Caldas

As a player, the younger Maximiliano was a defender for the Argentine national team and went to both the 1996 and 2004 Olympic Games. He retired due to injury, going on to coach in the Dutch Hoofdklasse, where he had been playing at the time. After working at club level, he became the assistant coach of the Dutch women's team for the 2006 Olympic Games, where the side won the gold medal. Caldas became the head coach in 2010, winning the 2012 Olympic hockey tournament, the 2013 World League and the 2014 World Cup, in the Hague. At the time of writing, Caldas is the head coach of Spain's men's team. He's in here, in no small part, due to his personality. He's a big man, with a strong personality. In pre and post match interviews he fills out the camera, but with that he brings a friendliness and, dare I say, a subtle sense of humour. He comes across as a big, brash teddy bear.

Ric Charlesworth

The second Australian on the list, he could have been on a list of iconic hockey players as well. Richard Ian Charlesworth is definitely somebody who has fulfilled his potential. Aside from hockey, he played A Grade cricket for Western Australia, worked as a doctor, after achieving a medical degree in 1976 and was elected to the Australian

Parliament in 1983, as the Federal Member for Perth, representing the Labor Party. After leaving politics Charlesworth became the head coach of the Australian women's hockey team in 1993. Here he oversaw an overwhelmingly successful period, spanning seven years. He managed the winning of four gold medals at the Champions Trophy, two World Cup victories and Olympic Games tournaments and the 1998 Commonwealth Games. Before taking on the head coaching role of the men's team in 2009, he was also a technical advisor to the Indian men's and women's national teams. With the Kookaburras he guided them to victory at the Champions Trophy three times, another Commonwealth Games title and two more World Cups, before resigning in 2014.

Since then Charlesworth has helped out his compatriot Alyson Annan with the Chinese national team, at the 2022 World Cup, 2023 Asian Games (where they were victorious) and the Paris 2024 Olympics, which saw the team claim a silver medal. Charlesworth has written several books, in one of them he described how the works of William Shakespeare has provided inspiration for him in his life and his coaching.

Roelant Oltmans

The Dutchman can easily be described as a journeyman. He is a well travelled hockey coach of international calibre, he's even worked as a technical director for football club NAC Breda. As the coach of the Netherlands women's squad, he led the side to World Cup victory in 1990. After moving across to the men's setup his team won the same competition in 1998. Since then, Oltmans has gone around the world. Aside from casting his eye over club sides Klein Zwitserland and Kampong, he has had stints with Pakistan (twice), India and Malaysia, as well as having returned to the Dutch men's team in 2005. His career has taken him to tournaments including the Sultan Azlan Shah Cup, the Commonwealth Games, Olympic Games, as well as the aforementioned World Cup. He is somebody that I would love to sit down with in a pub in order to pick his brains about coaching.

Roger Self OBE

The only British coach on this list, the Welshman had a strong impact on the current state of hockey within the UK. His crowning glory came at the 1988 Seoul Olympic Games, with the Great Britain's men winning the gold medal in the hockey tournament. This was done with an array of players from across the UK, all of whom were amateurs. This status of the players bought with it specific challenges and

Self was instrumental in arranging agreements with employers for time off for his squad when they were away on tour. A strong willed man, he additionally helped to create a structure that has led to the centralised system for English and British hockey players in order to challenge for international titles. The book Seoul Gold, by Rod Gilmour, goes into more detail and is well worth a read.

Horst Wein

A well rounded sporting connoisseur, the Hanover born Saxon turned his hand to a variety of games that included rugby, football, ice hockey and basketball, however, he is better known for his work in field hockey. The former German international player moved into coaching and the FIH labelled him one of the world's foremost experts in hockey and football development, before his death in 2016. The international governing body awarded Wein the first ever title of Master Coach, in 1975. Additionally, he worked for FC Barcelona, as well as the Spanish and German football federations and the International Olympic Committee. A pioneer of coaching techniques, he wrote a variety of books with a view on education and the sharing of ideas. In total he authored 36 pieces of sporting literature, including his well known piece, the Science of Hockey.

Recommended Reading

Athens to Athens, by David Miller

The Magic of Wembley; Women's Hockey Internationals 1951 - 1991, by Nan Williams and Christabel Russell Vick

Seoul Glow; the Story Behind Great Britain's 1988 Hockey Gold, by Rod Gilmour

Hockey, a Philosophical Game, by Andreu Enrich

The Science of Hockey, by Horst Wein

Shakespeare the Coach, by Ric Charlesworth

World's Best, by Ric Charlesworth

Pirates Punks and Politics; FC St. Pauli; Falling in Love with a Radical Football Club, by Nick Davidson

Relevant Websites

FIH - International Hockey Federation

The Hockey Museum

Half Court Press Magazine

Blackheath and Elthamians Hockey Club

Teddington Hockey Club

Printed in Great Britain
by Amazon

07ac5701-1c06-428d-a6e5-20cbf7b875cbR01